CAMPAIGN 265

FALL GELB 1940 (2)

Airborne assault on the Low Countries

DOUGLAS C DILDY   ILLUSTRATED BY PETER DENNIS

Series editor Marcus Cowper

OSPREY PUBLISHING
Bloomsbury Publishing Plc

PO Box 883, Oxford, OX1 9PL, UK
1385 Broadway, 5th Floor, New York, NY 10018, USA
Email: info@ospreypublishing.com

OSPREY is a trademark of Osprey Publishing, a division of
Bloomsbury Publishing Plc

© 2015 Osprey Publishing

First published in Great Britain in 2015 by Osprey Publishing

Transferred to digital print-on-demand in 2020

Printed and bound in Great Britain

ISBN: 978 1 4728 0274 3
PDF e-book ISBN: 978 14728 0275 0
e-Pub ISBN: 978 14728 0276 7

Editorial by Ilios Publishing Ltd, Oxford, UK (www.iliospublishing.com)
Index by Zoe Ross
Typeset in Myriad Pro and Sabon
Maps by Bounford.com
3D bird's-eye views by The Black Spot
Battlescene illustrations by Peter Dennis
Originated by PDQ Media, Bungay, UK

The Woodland Trust
Osprey Publishing supports the Woodland Trust, the UK's leading woodland
conservation charity.

www.ospreypublishing.com
To find out more about our authors and books visit our website. Here you
will find extracts, author interviews, details of forthcoming events and the
option to sign-up for our newsletter.

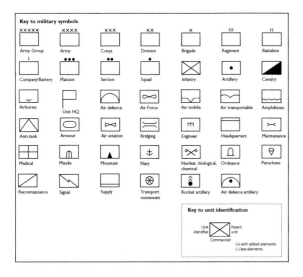

Key to military symbols

ARTIST'S NOTE

Readers may care to note that the original paintings from which the colour
plates in this book were prepared are available for private sale. The
Publishers retain all reproduction copyright whatsoever. All enquiries
should be addressed to:

Peter Dennis, Fieldhead, The Park, Mansfield, Notts, NG18 2AT, UK
Email: magie.h@ntlworld.com

The Publishers regret that they can enter into no correspondence upon this
matter.

ACKNOWLEDGEMENTS

The author is deeply indebted to a number of individuals who helped make
this book a thorough study of the epic tank battle at Hannut, Belgium, and
the airborne invasion of the Netherlands. Foremost was Belgian Army Major
Richard de Hennin whose immense knowledge of the tank battle and the
battlefield were indispensable in – for the first time in English – presenting
this account of the first major armoured clash in the history of warfare in a
clear and detailed manner. Also instrumental in this study were the historian
and French armoured cavalry expert Erik Barbanson, and noted Osprey
author Steve Zaloga, both of whom were extraordinarily helpful.

For their excellent support in locating and providing photographs of
French subjects, I am deeply indebted to Messieurs Alain Adam, Erik
Barbanson and retired French Army Colonel Max Schiavon. Alain Adam's
superb French World War II armour website www.chars-francais.net is
highly recommended for anyone, even non-French speakers. Likewise,
I thank Thijs Postma, Johann Schuurmann, and André Wilderdijk for their
generous provision of images of Dutch subjects, and to Daniel Brackx for
the Belgian ones. Thanks also go to Thomas Laemlein, Marc Romanych and
Gina McNeely for their outstanding support in providing a balanced
assortment of other compelling contemporary images.

Additionally, I am grateful to editor James V. Sanders, PhD, and fellow
Osprey authors Marc Romanych and Ryan Noppen, whose excellent critical
feedback make this concise discussion of these two significant military
campaigns far better than it could have otherwise been. Finally, I thank my
wonderful wife, Annette Dildy, for her enduring patience, limitless support,
and incredible inspiration, especially in the face of her recent life-
threatening illness. In light of the last-mentioned, series editor Marcus
Cowper's understanding and patience made completing this work possible,
and volume editor Nikolai Bogdanovic's expertise and his ability to refine
my lengthy and involved explanations into clear, concise statements will be
appreciated by the readers as well as their author.

AUTHOR'S NOTE

Central European Summer Time (CEST) was one hour ahead of French,
Belgian and British 'summertime', which was GMT/UTC+1 hour. The Dutch
used Amsterdamsche-tijd ('Amsterdam Time'), which was CEST-1:40 and
GMT/UTC-40 minutes. CEST is used throughout this work.

IMAGE CREDITS

IWM   Imperial War Museum
NARA   National Archives and Records Administration
NIMH   Netherlands Institute of Military History

CONTENTS

ORIGINS OF THE CAMPAIGN

The neutral states have assured us of their neutrality … This assurance is sacred to us and as long as no other nation violates their neutrality, we will also honour it with painstaking punctuality.

Adolf Hitler, 1 September 1939 – the day Germany invaded Poland

On 27 September 1939, only hours after the surrender of the Polish Army besieged at Warsaw, Adolf Hitler met with the commanders-in-chief of the three Wehrmacht services and announced his intention to invade France through 'Belgium and the Dutch appendix of Maastricht'. The Führer's objective was to reach the Channel coast in order 'to defeat … the French Army and the forces of the Allies fighting on their side, and at the same time to win as much territory as possible in Holland, Belgium, and Northern France, to serve as a base for successful prosecution of the war against

Hitler and his Oberkommando der Wehrmacht (OKW) and Oberkommando des Heeres (OKH) generals in conference at the planning map table. To Hitler's right is Franz Halder, the OKH chief of staff and architect of the *Fall Gelb* plan; to his immediate left is Generaloberst Walther von Brauchitsch, the chief of the army (OKH), with Generaloberst Wilhelm Keitel, the chief of the OKW, looking on. (IWM HU75533)

4

England'. He was anxious to quickly and decisively end the war that – on the Western front at least – had already expanded beyond his initial designs.

To achieve this aim and to do so before winter, in little more than three weeks the OKH (Oberkommando des Heeres, the army high command), under direction of General der Artillerie Franz Halder, developed *Aufmarschanweisung Fall Gelb* ('Deployment Directive, Case Yellow'). It was a hastily prepared improvisation calling for an offensive directly through Belgium and southern Holland, with the initial assaults swinging around the north and south sides of the fortress-ringed city of Liège before driving to the coast.

When the initial draft was issued on 19 October, it naturally employed only those German forces then arrayed in the West. Nine days earlier Generaloberst Fedor von Bock and his Heeresgruppe Nord (Army Group North) staff, fresh from their victorious conquest of northern Poland, arrived at Düsseldorf and was retitled Heeresgruppe B. Generaloberst Gerd von Rundstedt's Heeresgruppe A was established at Koblenz a fortnight later.

Three armies deployed along the German frontier opposite Belgium and southern Holland. After some reorganization these became, from north to south, Generaloberst Walter von Reichenau's Armeeoberkommando (AOK) 6, Generaloberst Günther Hans von Kluge's AOK 4, and General der Kavallerie Maximilian Freiherr von Weichs zu Glon's AOK 2. These were soon reinforced by General der Artillerie Georg von Küchler's AOK 18. In total these comprised 43 divisions, including nine panzer and four motorized infantry.

Heavily mechanized, Reichenau's AOK 6, followed by AOK 18, was to attack through the 'Maastricht Appendix' – the sliver of the Netherlands on the east bank of the Maas River, extending south between Belgium and Germany, just north of Liège – while Kluge's AOK 4, followed by AOK 12, was to bypass Liège to the south and then merge with Reichenau's army in central Belgium for the drive to the Channel coast. With another 22 infantry divisions, Heeresgruppe A was to provide flank coverage to the south.

Alarmed at the absence of Holland from the territory to be occupied, Luftwaffe Chief of Staff (COS) Generalmajor Hans Jeschonnek met with Hitler on 30 October to object that, 'if no Dutch territory is occupied, the English will take possession of Dutch airports'. Initially Hitler was unmoved, but 12 days later Jeschonnek was back, protesting that 'Holland must be occupied, because England

Luftwaffe Generalmajor Hans Jeschonnek, the chief of staff of the ObdL (Oberbefehlshaber der Luftwaffe), was the avid proponent for including the subjugation of the Netherlands, in its entirety, in the *Fall Gelb* plan. Once authorized, it was up to the Luftwaffe to devise the means – an airborne invasion – for its accomplishment. (NARA)

will violate Holland's air sovereignty and then we will not be able to protect the Ruhr area'. Constantly worried that the British might pre-empt his initiative by forcibly taking small neutral European nations into its sphere, Hitler ordered his personal military staff, the OKW, to direct the OKH to include the conquest of Holland in their *Fall Gelb* planning. At first, only the three divisions of AOK 18's X Armeekorps (AK) were assigned, but in the January modification to *Fall Gelb* Küchler's entire AOK 18 was given the mission to subjugate the Netherlands.

Meanwhile, the OKH recognized the difficulty of the proposed advance into Belgium, especially the crossings of the Meuse/Maas River. To secure bridgeheads and to place forces in the rear of the enemy, the Army staff added the Luftwaffe's neophyte, ad hoc airborne corps to land at Ghent and block Allied mobile forces, and to seize Meuse River crossings at Namur and Dinant, Belgium.

These revisions were under consideration when, on 10 January 1940, the airborne portion of the plan landed in the laps of the Belgian border forces – a Messerschmitt Bf 108 '*Taifun*' ('Typhoon') courier aircraft force-landed in error at Mechelen-sur-Meuse, on the Belgian side of the river. On board was Major Helmuth Reinberger, the commander of the Luftwaffe's *Fallschirmjäger* ('paratrooper') school at Stendal, who was carrying the entire 'airborne annex' of the *Fall Gelb* plan. Temporarily assigned as communications officer to Fliegerführer 220 (the Luftwaffe's coordinating HQ for airborne operations) to help integrate the Luftwaffe's air assault forces into the army's invasion plans, Reinberger was headed for a planning conference in Köln. To avoid the winter railway delays being experienced in the Ruhr, Major Erich Hoenmanns, a reserve officer in charge of camouflaging the small Loddenheide airfield near Münster, offered him a flight in a new *Taifun*. Against the stringent German security regulations, Reinberger accepted.

Approaching the Rhine, Hoenmanns encountered winter fog, wandered off course and when he attempted to switch fuel tanks, he accidentally shut off the fuel completely (this was only his second flight in a Bf 108), forcing a 'dead stick' landing on the west side of a wide river he thought was the Rhine. It was the Maas, and before Reinberger could destroy the contents of his dispatch case, both majors and the airborne plans for *Fall Gelb* were collected by Belgian police. Once Belgian King Léopold realized the papers' significance, to elicit guarantees of British and French assistance, a synopsis of the captured information was shared with the would-be allies.

The subsequent investigation, primarily involving the German military attaché's interview of the two majors in the Belgian jail, falsely assured the OKW that the 'dispatch case burned for certain'. Meanwhile, the entire concept of operations was under thorough reconsideration by Hitler, Halder, and the OKH staff. By 18 February it was so completely revised that it totally reversed the roles, dispositions and objectives of the German forces. Watching his plan unfolding in various 'command post exercises' Halder became convinced that Heeresgruppe A needed an additional, armoured army and, since the potential for a breakthrough was much greater by crossing the Meuse near Sedan than by assaulting the much more heavily defended Maas around Liège, the Panzers should be concentrated in the south, approaching through the Ardennes.

Meanwhile, Hitler, who had his own reservations, had just discussed the same concept with Generalleutnant Fritz Erich von Lewinski genannt von Manstein. When Halder presented the Führer with an entirely rewritten *Fall Gelb* plan which shifted the *Schwerpunkt* (main weight of the assault) to the south wing of the offensive, Hitler immediately ordered it implemented.

Under this revision, Heeresgruppe A became the main striking force with four armies totalling 45 divisions and 75 per cent of the Wehrmacht's mechanized forces. Heeresgruppe B's role was changed to providing a powerful and convincing feint, frequently referred to as the 'Matador's Cloak', as well as subjugating Holland. For these dual purposes Bock was left with two armies of 28 divisions, only three of which were armoured, and the Luftwaffe's small two-division airborne corps.

Bock's forces were divided between Reichenau's AOK 6, which was to cross the Maas and drive into Belgium, and Küchler's AOK 18, which was to subdue and occupy the Netherlands. The real question was how to use the new, untried weapon of Generalleutnant Kurt Student's ad hoc Luftlandekorps ('Air-Landing Corps').

With the shift of the *Schwerpunkt* to the south, airborne assaults at Ghent and the Meuse crossings became superfluous. Instead, after much discussion and debate, it was decided to use the *Fallschirmjäger* element (the paratroopers of the Luftwaffe's 7. Fliegerdivision) to seize the Maas and Rhine bridges, opening the 'back door' to the Dutch defensive redoubt, and to neutralize Fort Eben Emael, which guarded the bridges entering northern Belgium. Simultaneously, the air assault element (the army's specially trained 22. Luftlande Division) would be inserted into airfields surrounding The Hague in a bold *coup de main* (in German *strategischer Überfallen* or 'strategic assault') to quickly eliminate the Netherlands from the contest altogether.

On the western side of the front, some Allied leaders thought that Reinberger's plans were a deliberate Nazi plant. But to most they made perfect sense and confirmed their anticipation of a German drive across Belgium to outflank the Maginot Line. Convinced of this, the Allied Supreme Command worked hard to get the Belgians and Dutch to join in the collective defence and allow the establishment of strong defensive positions as far forward as possible. The two small nations, however, clung fiercely to their neutrality, fearful of provoking a German invasion and hoped that, when the inevitable occurred, the Allies would speedily come to their aid and assist in their defence. In all of this, the neutrals were naïve, the French were fooled, and the British were caught in a disaster not of their own making.

CHRONOLOGY

1939

1 September   Germany invades Poland, starting World War II in Europe.

3 September   Britain and France declare war on Germany.

10 September   The British Expeditionary Force (BEF) begins arriving in France.

27 September   OKW initial planning conference for the assault on the West.

9 October   Hitler's 'War Directive No. 6' orders the OKH to begin planning the invasion of northern France and the Low Countries.

19/29 October   OKH produces the original/revised *Fall Gelb* plan for the Western offensive.

14 November   OKW directive to OKH to include the conquest of Holland in *Fall Gelb* plan, amplified the following day with amending directive specifying an offensive up to the Dutch 'Grebbe Line'.

15 November   Général d'Armée Gamelin, Supreme Commander of Allied Armies, adopts the Dyle Plan designed to meet the German invasion in Belgium while the Maginot Line holds the French frontier.

20 November   Hitler's 'War Directive No. 8' orders the OKH planning to be flexible enough to shift the *Schwerpunkt* of *Fall Gelb* from Heeresgruppe B to Heeresgruppe A if an opportunity for greater success in the south presents itself.

1940

10 January   A German courier aircraft mistakenly lands near Mechelen, Belgium, and copies of the airborne portion of the *Fall Gelb* plan are captured.

25 January   *Fall Gelb* plan is revised to include the occupation of Holland, placing the panzer units on 24-hour notice, and emphasizing the need for surprise.

7, 14 February   Heeresgruppe A 'war games' convince OKH Chief of Staff General Halder that a major revision of the *Fall Gelb* plan is necessary.

18 February   Halder delivers to Hitler a completely rewritten draft OKH plan which places the *Schwerpunkt* of the attack through the Ardennes. Hitler orders the *Fall Gelb* directive to be changed accordingly.

24 February	Hitler signs the *Aufmarschanweisung Nr 4 Fall Gelb* deployment order.
20 March	Gamelin amends the 'Dyle Plan' with the 'Breda Variant' designed to join forces with the Dutch Army, thus forming a 'continuous front' from Holland to the Alps.
9 April	German naval units, army divisions, and Luftwaffe squadrons begin the invasion of Denmark and Norway.
10 May	*Fall Gelb* – the German invasion of the West – begins.
11 May	The BEF and French 1ère Armée begin to arrive at their positions on the Dyle Line.
12–13 May	The battle of Gembloux, focusing Allied attention in the north while German panzers approach through the Ardennes in the south.
13–14 May	The battle of Sedan – Guderian overwhelms unprepared French defences and turns west, heading for the Channel coast the next day.
18 May	BEF GHQ orders non-essential personnel evacuated from Boulogne, Calais and Dunkirk.
19 May	The BEF, French 1ère Armée, and Belgians establish a new defensive line on the Scheldt/Escaut River. Gamelin is replaced by Général Weygand as the Supreme Commander of Allied Forces. The BEF (Air Component – AC) evacuates to England.
20 May	Panzers reach the English Channel, encircling all Allied forces north of the Somme.
21 May	The BEF executes a 'spoiling attack' at Arras. Weygand meets with Général Billotte and King Léopold; Billotte is fatally injured in a car crash.
22 May	Panzers invest Calais and Boulogne.
23 May	Lord Gort orders the BEF to withdraw to Dunkirk.
24 May	Rundstedt again orders the panzers to halt; Hitler affirms the decision with OKW-directed *Haltbefehl*.
26 May	Operation *Dynamo* – the evacuation of the BEF from France – begins; Hitler rescinds *Haltbefehl*.
28 May	The Belgian Army surrenders.
31 May	The French 1ère Armée surrenders at Lille; 35,000 troops are captured.
4 June	The evacuation of Allied forces from Dunkirk ends; 35,000 French troops surrender.
5 June	*Fall Rot* – the final conquest of France – begins.
22 June	France signs an armistice with Germany.

OPPOSING COMMANDERS

GERMAN COMMANDERS

Once Hitler's new Reichsheer ('national army') began its unfettered expansion, 55-year-old **General der Infanterie Moritz Albrecht Franz Friedrich Fedor von Bock** was given command of Gruppenkommando 3 ('Army Group Command' – the precursor to the *Heeresgruppe*) at Dresden. Born into the Prussian military aristocracy in 1880 – and marrying a young Prussian noblewoman in 1905 – Bock was the archetype 'Prussian of the old school'. Commissioned in the prestigious 1. Garde-Regiment zu Fuß ('1st Imperial Foot Guards Regiment') in 1898, Bock soon attended the Preußische Kriegsakademie ('Prussian War College') and joined the General Staff, all before winning the coveted *Pour le Mérite* leading a battalion in World War I. He was tall, slim, and vigorous, with a dry, cynical sense of humour and an unbending military demeanour.

Generaloberst Fedor von Bock, commander of Heeresgruppe B. (Bundesarchiv Bild 146-1977-120-11)

Not a brilliant theoretician, instead Bock was very much a 'by the book' general. Promoted to *Generaloberst* on 15 March 1938, immediately after commanding the occupation of Austria, he then directed the subjugation of Czechoslovakia before leading Heeresgruppe Nord in the Polish campaign. After leading large fast-moving forces in three offensive actions, Bock was the perfect choice for commanding the disparate units – airborne, panzer, and infantry – in two separate and completely different, but simultaneous, operations.

Only four years Bock's junior, **Walter von Reichenau** was just a colonel working as chief of the Wehrmachtamt ('Ministry of Defence Staff' – which later morphed into Hitler's OKW) when Bock was first appointed army group commander. 'Exceptionally energetic and ambitious', Reichenau was one of the army's earliest and most outspoken supporters of Hitler and the Nazi Party. In fact, when Hitler came to power in 1933, Reichenau headed the Reichswehr chancellery and was instrumental in getting Nazi-sympathizer Werner von Blomberg appointed Reichswehrminister (Minister of Defence).

Subsequently ostracized by the Prussian elite, this Bohemian aristocrat – who had commanded artillery in World War I – opted for a transfer to command Wehrkreis VII ('Military District 7'). In the Polish campaign he led

AOK 10 and his 'audacious personal leadership and professional prowess was largely responsible for Heeresgruppe Süd's success'. Though appalled by Hitler's intent to violate Dutch and Belgian neutrality while invading France, the 'Nazi general' obediently accepted the assignment to do so.

Under Reichenau, **General der Kavallerie Erich Hoepner** – 'a very talented soldier and Guderian's chief rival for the leadership of the panzer arm' – led XVI AK (motorisiert, abbreviated 'mot.') in the invasion of Poland. Born in Brandenburg in 1886, Hoepner was commissioned as a cavalry officer in 1906 and fought in World War I, reaching the rank of *Rittmeister* (cavalry captain). Two years afterwards he participated in the Kapp-Lüttwitz putsch, a failed military coup attempting to overthrow the newly formed Weimar government, but proved to be an early opponent of Nazism.

Often called *Der Alte Reiter* ('the old cavalryman'), Hoepner was an early advocate of mechanization and commanded the 1. Lichtedivision ('light division') during its transition from horses to panzers. Afterwards, he was Guderian's successor to command XVI AK (mot.), leading it into Prague during the occupation of Czechoslovakia and – commanding the 1. and 4. Panzer and two infantry divisions – proved hugely successful in the Polish campaign.

Generaloberst Walter von Reichenau. (Bundesarchiv Bild 183-B05284)

The youngest German general commanding major forces in Heeresgruppe B's operations was from Germany's youngest military service – **Luftwaffe Generalleutnant Kurt Arthur Benno Student**. Born 12 May 1890 in the Prussian province of Brandenburg, Student was commissioned as an infantry lieutenant in 1911, but two years later he joined the fledgling Imperial German Flying Corps, eventually commanding Jagdstaffel 9 and ending the war with seven confirmed victories. During the Weimar years he became an avid glider enthusiast and was sent to observe the Soviet Union's Red Army air manoeuvres each year between 1924 and 1928, where he first witnessed parachute operations.

LEFT
General der Kavallerie Erich Hoepner. (Bundesarchiv Bild 146-1971-068-10)

RIGHT
General Kurt Student, commander of the Luftlandekorps. (Bundesarchiv Bild 146-1979-128-26)

After joining the newly established, still-secret Luftwaffe in 1934, he was appointed Inspekteur der Fliegerschule, with specific instructions to coordinate the development of his embryonic parachute, glider, and air-landing troops. When Luftwaffe chief Hermann Göring combined these disparate elements into the small, rather roughly organized 7. Flieger Division, he made Student (now *Generalmajor*) its commander. The next year Göring appropriated the army's air-landing regiment and anticipated the formation of the Luftlandekorps by appointing Student as Inspekteur des Fallschirm-und-Luftlandetruppe.

FRENCH COMMANDERS

The Supreme Commander of all Allied land forces was the Chief of the General Staff of National Defence, **Général d'Armée Maurice Gustave Gamelin**. 'Not a leader of men', Gamelin fancied himself a 'philosopher general' who managed resources and composed detailed plans to do so. In charge of actually 'running the war' was **Général d'Armée Alphonse-Joseph Georges**; his role as commander of Théâtre d'Operations du Nord-Est (TONE) was to coordinate the operations of three Army Groups stretching from the Channel coast to the Swiss border, apportion the air force effort supporting them, and direct the assignment of army reserves.

The most critical part of the front – at least from Gamelin and Georges's perspectives – was entrusted to 65-year-old **Général d'Armée Gaston-Henri Gustave Billotte**. A big, bluff, hearty man, Billotte graduated from Saint-Cyr military academy in 1896 and was commissioned in the naval infantry. He served mostly in Indochina and by 1930 was made the chief of French forces there. Returning to France, he became an advocate for modernization and was credited with persuading the army's top authorities to create the first two cavalry tank divisions. When the two allies declared war, he was made commander of Groupe d'Armées 1, controlling the French armies arrayed from Lille to Longuyon. However, he viewed the British and Belgians only as allies fighting alongside and refused to accept responsibility for their direction, actions, or consequences.

Général d'Armée Gaston-Henri Gustave Billotte. (Getty Images)

Commanding France's strongest military formation – the powerful and mobile 1ère Armée – was **Général d'Armée Jean Georges Maurice Blanchard**, an artillery expert who had graduated from the École Polytechnique in 1899. During World War I he served in frontline positions, winning two citations before being assigned to Marshal Joffre's staff. Promoted rapidly through the general officer ranks in the 1930s, Blanchard was a smart, astute, and studious leader with a scientific approach to solving military problems, and in 1938 he became the director of all higher military education.

Later replacing Blanchard was **Général de Corps d'Armée René-Jacques-Adolphe Prioux**. He was a cavalryman in the truest, most traditional sense of the word, but

once acceptance of motorized and mechanized vehicles could no longer be avoided, Prioux became one of France's most talented and resourceful cavalry commanders and was the logical choice to direct the French Army's only armoured corps. Adhering completely to the cavalry side of the French Army's schizophrenic armour doctrine, he used his tanks as he had horse-mounted cavalry – as screens, for reconnaissance and in mounted charges.

LEFT
Général d'Armée Jean Georges Maurice Blanchard. (Max Schiavon)

RIGHT
Général de Corps d'Armée René-Jacques-Adolphe Prioux (Max Schiavon)

BRITISH COMMANDERS

Born John Standish Surtees Prendergast Vereker in Ireland in 1886, the leader of the British forces in France was the 6th Viscount Gort of Limerick; he entered the British Army in 1905 as **Lord Gort**. After completing his education at Harrow, he was commissioned in the Grenadier Guards Regiment and during World War I, as a battalion commander, he was wounded four times, being awarded the Victoria Cross (VC) and two Distinguished Service Orders (DSOs).

British General Lord Gort with generals Dill and Brooke. (IWM F2027)

A large, burly man, Lord Gort was the inspiring visage of a born fighter and was selected as the new Chief of the Imperial General Staff (CIGS), being 'jumped' over several more senior generals in doing so. Once the war began, he was given the coveted command of the British Expeditionary Force (BEF) to France. Despite many disingenuous characterizations made previously, Gort proved to be a decisive leader, even if his methods were entirely conventional.

BELGIAN COMMANDERS

The Belgian Army Chief of the General Staff (CGS) from 1935 through 1939, **Lieutnant-General Édouard Van den Bergen** was responsible for defence planning up through the 'Mechelen Incident'. During this episode Van den Bergen aggressively brought his army to full alert, recalled 80,000 troops from winter leave through a nationwide radio broadcast, and opened the frontier barriers along the French border to allow the Allies unimpeded entry – all without the king's consent. Constitutionally, the King of the Belgians was the army's commander-in-chief and the 39-year-old monarch took umbrage to his CGS's unilateral actions; by the end of January 1940 he had forced his resignation and reassigned him to command V Corps.

Educated at Eton and Ghent University, **King Léopold III** had been on the throne only six years and, although he had seen action as a private in the 12ème Régiment during World War I, he could hardly be considered experienced in military matters.

Léopold's aide-de-camp (ADC) and chief military advisor was **Lieutnant-General Raoul van Overstraeten**. Entering the École Royale Militaire ('Royal Military Academy') in 1902 and graduating into the horse artillery, by 1914 Overstraeten was a Cavalry Division staff officer fighting against the German invasion of World War I, and later in the successful East African campaign. Afterwards he rose to command the horse artillery, was the ADC for the Minister of Defence, and commanded the École de Guerre ('War College') before being chosen as Léopold's ADC.

DUTCH COMMANDERS

The Dutch people were ruled by the popular 60-year-old **Queen Wilhelmina**. The Netherlands' monarch since she was 18, Wilhelmina led the Dutch through their successful neutrality during World War I and had no sanguine view of the disturbing political and military developments in neighbouring Germany. Dissatisfied with most of her governments, who were always eager

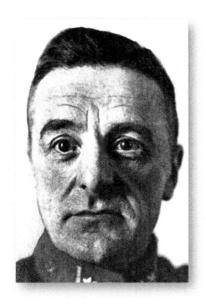

Dutch Generaal Henri Gerard Winkelman. (Ryan Noppen)

to cut the military budget, Wilhelmina was known as a 'soldier's queen', desiring a small but well trained and equipped army.

Being a woman, constitutionally Wilhelmina could not be Supreme Commander, and when the Dutch Army began its general mobilization in August 1939, this responsibility was invested in the CGS **Generaal Izaak H. Reijnders**. However, Reijnders resigned six months later when the government disagreed with his attempts to establish a continuous defensive line by extending the southern flank to join the Belgians and refused funding for his construction of modern fortifications in both the main and secondary defensive lines.

Replacing Reijnders was 64-year-old retired **Generaal Henri Gerard Winkelman**. An infantry officer who graduated from the Royal Military Academy in Breda in 1896, in the mid-1930s Winkelman commanded the 4e Divisie before retiring when he was passed over for the CGS position. Elderly and entirely conventional, Winkelman based his defence on the traditional Dutch system of static positions behind rivers, canals, inundations, and other water barriers.

OPPOSING PLANS

The objective of offensive 'Yellow' is to deny Holland and Belgium to the English by swiftly occupying them; [and] to defeat, by an attack through Belgium and Luxembourg territory, the largest possible forces of the Anglo-French army.

Führer Directive Nr. 10 for the Conduct of the War, 24 February 1940

FALL GELB PLAN

Fall Gelb was a detailed deployment order designed to launch the initial phase of Hitler's campaign to eliminate the Western democracies from the European conflict. It was the first of a series of operations – the second one being *Fall Rot* ('Case Red'), which would result in the conquest of France – and it consisted of four parallel (near simultaneous) branches:

1. Vigorous attacks against the Maginot Line by Leeb's Heeresgruppe C in order to pin the 24 divisions of 'interval troops' (including the British 51st 'Highland' Division) to their positions and thus prevent them from being used to attack the southern flank of the German breakthrough.
2. The airborne invasion of the Netherlands by the Luftwaffe's Luftlandekorps with ground relief provided by Küchler's AOK 18.
3. The strong advance through central Belgium by Reichenau's AOK 6, designed to convince the Allied command that it was the main thrust.
4. The advance through Luxembourg and southern Belgium by the armoured formations of Rundstedt's Heeresgruppe A to achieve a major breakthrough between Sedan, France, and Dinant, Belgium.

While the last listed depended heavily on how convincing the third was – Heeresgruppe B's 'Matador's Cloak' – the second was a separate and unique operation, known by its own operational designation: *Unternehmen* 'F' ('Operation "F"', 'F' for '*Festung*', German for 'fortress', i.e. 'Fortress Holland').

The quickest way to eliminate the Dutch from the Allies' order of battle – and exorcise the anxiety of the RAF using Dutch airfields to raid the Ruhr – was by what we now call 'decapitation' – that is, the neutralization, by lethal means if necessary, of the enemy's leadership, command, and control. In this case, it would be the role of Generalleutnant Hans Graf von Sponeck's 22. Luftlande Division to insert some 6,500 troops – known as Gruppe Nord

The Wehrmacht's secret weapon for the invasion of the Low Countries. Although their potential was revealed in the April invasion of Denmark and Norway, the Allies had no appreciation for the shock effect of Student's *Fallschirmjäger*. (IWM MH8059)

– at three airfields around The Hague, then enter the Dutch capital to capture Queen Wilhelmina, the Cabinet, and the High Command, thereby securing their capitulation.

In addition to securing the three airfields for the air-landing troops, Student's 7. Fliegerdivision – the bulk of which formed Gruppe Süd – would secure the bridges spanning the tangle of rivers that formed the south side of 'Fortress Holland' and Waalhaven airfield at Rotterdam, opening the way for a motorized corps to relieve the lightly armed air assault forces. In short, the Germans intended to conquer Holland using the largest and most ambitious airborne assault thus far in the history of warfare.

The 'Matador's Cloak' was larger, but much less involved. Reichenau's AOK 6 was to assault the Belgian defences along the Maas with five infantry corps, using Student's detached glider-borne assault battalion ('Sturmabteilung Koch' or 'assault unit Koch') to seize three bridges near Maastricht and neutralize Fort Eben Emael. Once this 'door' had been 'kicked in', Hoepner's XVI AK (mot.) would drive deep into central Belgium, heading for the open space between the Dyle and Meuse rivers known as the 'Gembloux Gap'. If the Allies 'took the bait', the panzers and the trailing infantry corps would be met by the Allies' best mobile forces – the BEF and the French 1ère Armée – thus preventing them from being able to respond to Heeresgruppe A's panzers approaching Sedan through the thickly forested hills of the Ardennes.

THE FRENCH 'PLAN D'

Tragically for all the democracies involved, Gamelin planned to do exactly what the Germans hoped. From the scant, secret, cursory contacts with the Belgian Army staff in November 1939, Gamelin knew that their preferred main line of defence was along the Albert Canal and Maas River, extending in a large salient from Antwerp to Liège to Namur. However, Gamelin also knew that his mobile forces could not reach this line before German mechanized units overwhelmed the Belgian infantry defending it.

Therefore, Gamelin decided on an intermediate – and shorter and straighter – defensive line from Antwerp through Louvain and Wavre to Namur, Givet, and Sedan. He calculated that two of his three motorized armies, the 1ère Armée and the BEF, could reach this line and establish an effective defence, provided

The Albert Canal provided an imposing and formidable water barrier against invasion from the east, provided its steep banks were adequately defended. Belgian 'strict neutrality' forfeited the opportunity to have the substantial Allied forces stop Hitler's aggression at this very advantageous point. (Author's collection)

the Belgians held the Germans at the Albert Canal–Maas Line for four to seven days. Because the Louvain–Wavre section of the line was anchored on a small stream generously named the Dyle River, Gamelin's deployment order was called 'Plan D'.

The Allies' third motorized formation, Général Giraud's 7e Armée, formed the main element of the Réserve du GQG (GQG reserve). Initially positioned around Reims, Giraud would have been able to support either Général Gaston Billotte's Groupe d'Armées 1 along the Dyle–Meuse Line or Général André-Gaston Prételat's Groupe d'Armées 2 behind the Maginot fortresses.

Just south of Louvain, the 'Dyle River' is a stream only seven yards/metres wide – not a particularly imposing terrain feature to aid the defence. (Author's collection)

However, in the early springtime Gamelin became worried that the Allied plan needlessly sacrificed the Netherlands. Believing that including the small Dutch Army in the Allies' overall defensive array would force the Germans to divert forces to their northern flank, Gamelin detailed his mobile reserve to link up with the Dutch north-east of Antwerp, at Breda. Consequently, Giraud's 7e Armée was transferred to the far north end of the Allied line, a position from which it would race to Breda, thus making it unavailable to counter any German breakthroughs, wherever they might occur.

On 20 March the 'Dyle Plan-Breda Variant' was issued – effectively sealing the fates of Billotte's northern two armies and the BEF, and with them, the destinies of France, Belgium, and the Netherlands.

BELGIAN DEFENSIVE PLANS

The basis of the Belgian defences facing Germany was formed by the Albert Canal, running from Antwerp to join the Maas/Meuse River near Maastricht, the Netherlands, then following the Meuse from Liège to Namur. This was a naturally powerful defensive line with imposing water barriers and the eastern end of this salient was capped by 12 formidable forts surrounding Liège, with another seven at Namur. This was considered 'a very strong position and the natural obstacles were reinforced with a large number of fortifications and earthworks'.

However, the salient ran over 160 miles (260km) and the Belgians' 20 divisions would be stretched thin defending it, so Allied reinforcement was necessary. But 'owing to its distance from the French frontier, no Franco-British help could be expected' before it would have been penetrated by the Germans, and once the invader was through one flank of the salient, they would be in the rear of its other, causing wholesale collapse.

Instead, relying on French and British assistance, Van den Bergen decided that the main line of defence should be a relatively straight line connecting Antwerp and Namur. This line running through Koningshooikt–Malines–Louvain–Wavre was known as the K-W Ligne and generally conformed to Gamelin's 'Dyle Line'. Beginning late in 1939, it was fortified with 'a large number of works spread over several lines, protected by an anti-tank barrier

The Allied 'Plan Dyle', the Belgian and Dutch defensive plans, and Heeresgruppe B's initial movements in *Fall Gelb*, 10 May 1940.

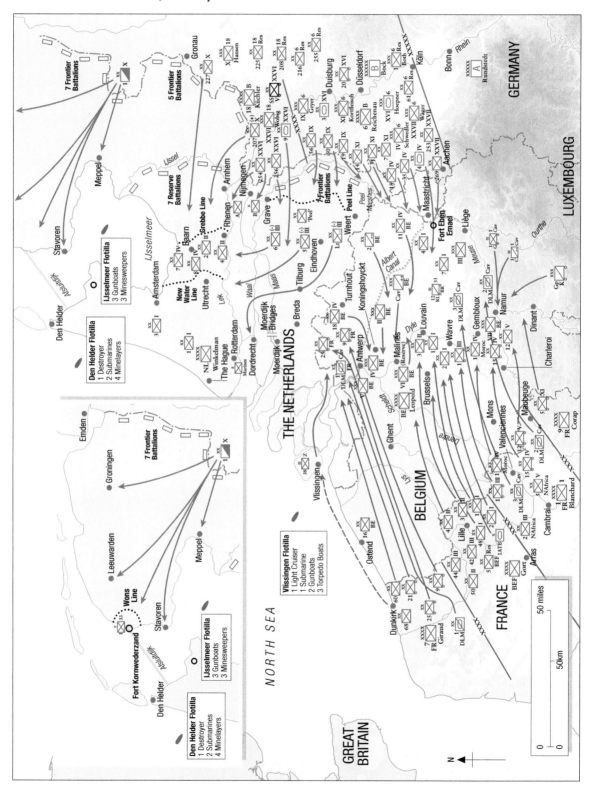

and arrangements for flooding … [backed by an] underground telephone system and a dedicated road network'. Even without formal coordination, Van den Bergen expected the BEF and French 1ère Armée to arrive at these positions on the third day.

'FORTRESS HOLLAND' – THE DUTCH DEFENSIVE PLAN

The small, weakly trained and poorly equipped Dutch Veldleger ('field army') was patently inadequate to defend the 200-mile (322km) long Dutch-German border, so Winkelman employed the traditional *Vesting Holland* ('Fortress Holland') concept, protecting the heart of the nation containing The Hague, Amsterdam, Rotterdam, and Utrecht. He concentrated the bulk of the Veldleger (IIe and IVe Legerkorps) along the 25-mile (40km) long, heavily wooded ridge running from Baarn, near the IJsselmeer coast, to Rhenen on the Lek River. Strengthened with earthworks studded with concrete bunkers, casemates with steel-cupolas, and pillboxes, and protected by a continuous anti-tank (A/T) ditch and the inundated Gelder Valley, this was a formidable defensive position. It was anchored at the Lek on an imposing, fortified hill called the Grebbeberg, thus the army's front was known as the 'Grebbe Line'.

Between the Lek and the Maas rivers, Winkelman deployed two independent infantry brigades and south of the Maas he positioned a large screening force (IIIe Legerkorps) to delay the German forces along the 37.5-mile (60km) long Grave–Peel–Weert line (called the 'Peel Line'). To prevent this line being outflanked from the south (through Belgium), the Lichte Divisie ('Light Division', the Veldleger's only mobile formation) was initially echeloned in the Tilburg–Eindhoven area, able to react quickly in any direction.

Believing that no 'Allied forces could arrive [in southern Holland] in time to close the gap south of Weert', Winkelman directed that, in the event of a major German attack, IIIe Legerkorps was to withdraw northwards, behind the Waal, and the Lichte Divisie would move to Rotterdam. Ie Legerkorps was held in reserve and guarded the rear areas against seaborne landings and airborne assaults.

Like the French and Belgians, the Dutch put great stock in fixed fortifications, building approximately 2,000 pillboxes and casemates, but mostly in thin lines along the borders and rivers. The only defence in depth was the Grebbe Line fortifications, seen here during the winter before the onslaught. (NIMH)

OPPOSING FORCES

A strategic surprise attack on our country will be coupled with a surprise attack from the air, in which military as well as civilian aircraft will be used to transport troops that could land on our major airfields.

Generaal Izaak H. Reijnders, Chief of the Dutch General Staff, September 1938

GERMAN FORCES

Heeresgruppe A
The invasion of the Netherlands was spearheaded by the Luftwaffe's small, elite 7. Fliegerdivision. Its Fallschirmjäger Regiment 1 (FJR 1) comprised three battalions, the first of which (I./FJR 1) had combat experience in the assault on Denmark and Norway just the previous month. FJR 2 had two battalions, only one of which (I./FJR 2) had completed parachute training. The division also included 'Sturmabteilung Koch' – the special glider-borne assault battalion committed to attack the Belgian fortress Eben Emael and the Albert Canal bridges – and an assault gun battery with four old Skoda GebK15 75mm mountain guns, plus a company each of 2cm FlaK 38 and 3.7cm PaK 36 guns, as well as medical, reconnaissance, and signals companies.

FJR 1 formed the basis of Gruppe Süd; its mission was to secure the bridges across the three main waterways – the 'Hollandsch Diep' at Moerdijk, the 'Oude Maas' at Dordrecht, and the 'Nieuwe Maas' at Rotterdam – and to seize Waalhaven airfield at Rotterdam. FJR 2 was the initial assault force for Gruppe Nord; its mission was to parachute onto the three airfields around The Hague – Ypenburg, Valkenburg, and Ockenburg – and secure them for the arrival of 22. Luftlande Division.

Sponeck's 22. Luftlande Division consisted of three infantry regiments, one pioneer company, a bicycle reconnaissance squadron, and the medical and signal battalions trained to be delivered to the battle area by Junkers Ju 52/3m transports. Infanterie-Regiment 16 (IR 16) was to land at Waalhaven and capture Rotterdam while the other two regiments (IR 47 and 65), a pioneer company, communications company, bicycle squadron, and motorcycle messenger section – some 6,500 troops – would land at the three airfields around The Hague. The units landing at Valkenburg and Ockenburg were to establish blocking positions while the main force, landing at Ypenburg, would enter the city and capture Queen Wilhelmina, her Cabinet and Winkelman's High Command.

The ground advance – designed to both fix the Veldleger in static positions north of the rivers and, south of them, penetrate deep to relieve the airborne troops – was the task of Küchler's AOK 18. It consisted of nine divisions, including the 9. Panzer-Division, the Waffen-SS's 'Verfügungs' ('Expeditionary') motorized division, six second-line infantry divisions and the only horse-mounted cavalry division in the German Army. Generalleutnant Christian Hansen's X AK (with the 1. Kavallerie-Division covering the northern flank) would advance in strength north of the Rhine to engage

Paratroopers unloading a BMW of Leutnant Geyer's *Kradschützenzug* (motorcycle platoon) from a I./KGzbV 1 Ju 52/3m tri-motor transport. (NIMH)

the Veldleger on the Grebbe Line. Generalleutnant Albert Wobig's XXVI AK would cross the Maas between Nijmegen and Maastricht and penetrate the Peel Line, opening the way for the 9. Panzer-Division to race westwards to the paratroop-held bridges leading to Rotterdam.

Commanded by Generalleutnant Dr Alfred Ritter von Hubicki, 9. Panzer-Division was originally the Austrian Army's Schnelle Division ('fast division'), absorbed into the Wehrmacht following the *Anschluss* ('annexation') in 1938, and redesignated the 4. Lichtedivision. As the newest panzer unit (established 4 January 1940) it was also the smallest, with only two battalions in each regiment, and was primarily equipped with surplus training tanks – 84 PzKpfw Is and IIs – with only 41 PzKpfw III battle tanks and 16 PzKpfw IV 'bunker-busters' ('*bunkerknacker*').

As the 'Matador's Cloak', Reichenau's AOK 6 – five corps containing two panzer and 18 infantry divisions – was on a completely separate and independent mission. The breakthrough thrust would be driven through Maastricht and across the Albert Canal by Generalmajor Johann Joachim Stever's 4. Panzer-Division, initially assigned to IV AK. Once the door to Belgium was 'kicked in', Hoepner's XVI AK (mot.) would move forward, Generalmajor Horst Stumpff's 3. Panzer-Division taking its position on Stever's right flank, and Hoepner would take control of both units for the diversionary thrust into central Belgium.

Panzers on the Belgian plain: Hoepner's XVI AK (mot.) possessed 486 small, machine gun-armed PzKpfw I (foreground) and 20mm cannon-armed PzKpfw II light tanks – plus 120 PzKpfw III/IV mediums – for its role as the 'Matador's Cloak' in the *Fall Gelb* campaign. (NARA)

The two panzer units were amongst the five originals, but due to the demands of the *Panzerwaffen*'s frenetic expansion, they were the slowest to upgrade, still outfitted according to the March 1939 organizational tables. Consequently, the four tank regiments each contained only 20 PzKpfw IIIs and a dozen PzKpfw IVs. However, between them they had 252 PzKpfw Is (machine-gun armed) and 234 PzKpfw II (20mm cannon) old light tanks. Because it was nearly impossible to distinguish individual tank types at a

distance, especially from the air, these two divisions – with 606 panzers, plus command vehicles, armoured cars and half-track personnel carriers – were perfect for creating the impression of a major mechanized offensive into the Belgian plain.

The Luftwaffe

Supporting both of Bock's armies was General der Flieger Albert Kesselring's Luftflotte 2 ('Air Fleet 2'), composed of a special-purpose command to support *Unternehmen 'F'*, a long-range bomber command (Fliegerkorps IV) to interdict Allied forces advancing into Holland and Belgium, and a close-support command (Fliegerkorps VIII) to provide the 'flying artillery' assisting Reichenau's thrust into central Belgium, as well as an air defence command.

Generalmajor Richard Putzier's Fliegerkorps zbV (Fliegerkorps zur besonderen Verwendung – 'Flying Corps for Special Missions' – formerly Fliegerführer 220) was assigned six *Kampfgruppen* ('battle groups', meaning bomber groups) totalling 149 combat-ready He 111s and 21 new Ju 88s. Attached to Putzier's command was also a *gruppe* of 37 Stuka dive-bombers (IV.(St)/LG 1 from StG 77) to support Student's Gruppe Süd.

Supporting Reichenau's advance into central Belgium was Kesselring's two other *Fliegerkorps*. General der Flieger Alfred Keller's Fliegerkorps IV would concentrate on long-range targets, such as Allied airfields, rear-area depots, and the railway system, using 135 serviceable He 111H/Ps and 86 Ju 88As. Generalmajor Wolfram von Richthofen's Fliegerkorps VIII would provide battlefield interdiction and close air support, employing six *Stukagruppen*, with 198 Ju 87Bs, a *Schlachtgruppe* ('assault group') of 38 Hs 123A biplanes and a *Kampfgeschwader* ('bomber wing' or KG) of 83 Do 17Z light bombers, as well as 115 Bf 109Es to provide fighter coverage for the panzers and Stukas.

Air superiority would be assured by Generalmajor Hans von Döring's Jagdfliegerführer 2 ('Fighter Command 2' or Jafü 2) providing 233 Bf 109s and 92 Bf 110s tasked with 'the sole mission of providing air cover for the air transport action and the air landings [in a] carefully calculated schedule that guaranteed an uninterrupted air umbrella'.

ALLIED FORCES

The French 1ère and 7e Armées

Bock's Heeresgruppe B faced two French infantry-based formations, plus similarly organized BEF, Belgian and Dutch armies. But unlike their two defending armies stationed on the Meuse south of Namur, 1ère and 7e Armées were the most mobile and powerful commands in the French Army.

Général Blanchard's 1ère Armée consisted of seven infantry divisions – all active duty; three of them were motorized and three others were the best colonial divisions in France. They would be screened by the rapid forward deployment of Général Prioux's elite Corps de Cavalerie. Consisting of two powerful armoured cavalry divisions – the 2e and 3e Divisions Légère Mécanique (DLM) – this was the only command in the Allied array remotely resembling a German panzer corps.

The French had two distinctly different armoured formations and doctrines: the heavy, slow, infantry-support Divisions Cuirassée (DCr, or 'armoured divisions') and the cavalry arm's well-balanced, fast, and powerful DLMs (often mistakenly called 'light mechanized divisions', these were actually – according to both French grammar and army doctrine – 'mechanized light divisions', the term 'light' being used in European armies of the 1920s–40s to indicate units that were more mobile than regularly and more heavily equipped ones). The Corps de Cavalerie was established on 26 December 1939, initially concentrating the 1ère and 2e DLMs under one command. The newly formed 3e DLM, composed primarily of recalled horse cavalry reservists, was assigned to Prioux's

corps on 26 March when the 1ère DLM was siphoned off to join Giraud's 7e Armée to participate in Gamelin's 'Breda Variant'. All three DLMs were nearly identically equipped, consisting of an armoured brigade of two tank regiments supported by motorized infantry, reconnaissance, and artillery regiments, as well as lorried engineer, communications, medical, supply, and transportation companies.

A French SOMUA S35 cavalry tank of the 18e Regiment de Dragons (1ère DLM) undergoing maintenance at its base in Reims, March 1938. (Erik Barbanson)

Typically a French armoured squadron consisted of 21 tanks (compared with 16–18 PzKpfw III/IVs in Hoepner's panzer companies) and were organized in pairs: two squadrons forming a group (battalion) and two groups forming a regiment, totalling 84 tanks. Due to the shortage of SOMUA (Société d'Outillage Mécanique et d'Usinage d'Artillerie) S35 cavalry tanks, half of the squadrons were equipped with Hotchkiss H35/39 light infantry-support tanks.

The SOMUA S35 was specifically designed to meet the French cavalry's requirements for a fast, long-ranged and powerfully armed and armoured tank able to operate in the arm's traditional roles of reconnaissance, screening, and mounted charges. Powered by a 190hp SOMUA V-8 petrol engine, the 21.4-ton vehicle could travel 143 miles (230km) at up to 25mph (40km/h). It mounted an excellent high-velocity 47mm SA 35 L/34 cannon and coaxial Reibel 7.5mm M31 machine gun in an electrically powered turret and was protected by 35–40mm (1.37–1.57in.) of hull armour and 45–55mm (1.77–1.97in.) on the turret. However, the otherwise superior design was hamstrung by the French penchant for small cast turrets (where the tank commander also operated the vehicle's guns) and lack of radios at the platoon level.

Including command vehicles, each DLM had 88 S35s, supported by 87 H35/39s, in their 'combat brigades'. Each division also contained a reconnaissance regiment of 40 Panhard 178 armoured cars and a motorized infantry regiment of 3,088 truck-mounted troops with organic armour – 63 Renault AMR 33/35 or Hotchkiss H35/39 infantry-support tanks – and a dozen 25mm A/T guns. (The AMR 33/35 was a six-ton machine-gun armed tankette, of which only 320 were produced; due to a lack of these, the 3e DLM's motorized infantry was equipped with 22 H35s and 47 H39s.) The unit's reinforced motorized artillery provided 24 light (75mm) and 24 medium (105mm) guns, eight 47mm A/T guns and a small battery of 25mm AA guns. Altogether, Prioux's cavalry corps was more than a match for Hoepner's XVI AK (mot.).

'On an independent mission' – attempting to link with the Dutch forces at Breda – was Giraud's 7e Armée. This was a smaller version of Blanchard's 1ère Armée, consisting of the 1ère DLM, three motorized infantry and two 'leg' infantry divisions, one of which had recently been formed from naval infantry battalions stationed along the coast.

The British Expeditionary Force

The British contribution to 'Plan D' was for seven infantry divisions to establish a defence in depth between Louvain and Wavre, with a motorized reconnaissance unit screening to the east and the 1st Army Tank Brigade (1st ATB), as well as two mechanized reconnaissance brigades, in reserve. Two Territorial (reservist) divisions and three divisions of untrained 'lines of communications troops' would be left in France.

While not 'motorized infantry' in the technical sense, each of the BEF's three corps had sufficient motor transport to move one division each day. These were generously supported by 2,472 artillery pieces – a huge number by any measure – but they were almost exclusively ancient World War I (and prior) weapons.

Gort's fastest reconnaissance element was the 12th Battalion of the Royal Lancers (12th RL), driving 38 Morris CS9 armoured cars. His two 'light armoured reconnaissance' brigades each had 56 tiny, 5-ton, machine gun-armed Vickers Mark VIb tankettes and 88 Universal Carriers. The only real armour possessed by the BEF was two Royal Tank Regiment (RTR) battalions forming the 1st ATB. Of the 100 infantry-support tanks in these units, just 23 were 26.5-ton Matilda Mark IIs mounting a 2-pounder (40mm) cannon and having 75mm armour – an opponent superior to Hoepner's PzKpfw IIIs – but the rest were machine gun-armed 12-ton Matilda Is, supported by a dozen Vickers tankettes and 16 Universal Carriers.

Allied air power

Air support for the two French armies and the BEF was organized to provide only aerial reconnaissance and fighter cover – there was no dedicated offensive air power. Battlefield observation was provided by Westland Lysander (five squadrons) and Mureaux 115/117 (eight escadrilles) army cooperation observation aircraft. Tactical reconnoitring was provided by Bristol Blenheim (four squadrons) and Potez 63.11 (two squadron-sized 'groups') twin-engine reconnaissance aircraft.

Providing defensive air cover for Blanchard's and Giraud's armies was Armée de l'Air ('Army of the Air' or AdA) Groupements de Chasse 23 and 25 – four fighter groups containing 71 mixed-construction Morane-Saulnier (MS) 406s and 26 of the more modern, all-metal – but under-gunned – American-built Curtiss Hawk 75s. The BEF's Air Component (AC) had four fighter squadrons totalling 48 Hawker Hurricanes, plus 22 Gloster Gladiator biplanes in the two units re-equipping with the Hurricane.

BEF machine gun-armed Matilda I infantry tanks of the 4th Battalion, Royal Tank Regiment 'undergoing maintenance' for the benefit of the photographer. (IWM O747)

The Hurricane was a modern design that fell somewhere between the two AdA fighter types: its mixed construction made it heavy, slow, and less manoeuvrable but it mounted an eight-gun battery. However, the real difference between the Allied types and the Luftwaffe's excellent – fast, all-metal, and heavily armed – Bf 109E was that the latter employed the extremely flexible and lethal four-aircraft *schwarm* formation and tactics, while the Allies (and the neutrals) were still wedded to the outdated, ineffective and terribly vulnerable three-fighter 'vics' and *patrouilles* ('patrols').

NEUTRAL FORCES

The Belgians

Historically a well-trodden military thoroughfare between France and Germany, Belgium invested in a relatively strong, defensively orientated army. In peacetime it comprised 126,800 men organized into six infantry, two cavalry and four reserve divisions, plus the Chasseurs Ardennais (ChA) light infantry and two fortress systems at Liège and Namur. Mobilized on 26 August 1939, the army swelled to 22 divisions. Although manpower had reached 600,000 troops by May 1940, over half of these were still in training.

Belgian infantry divisions were relatively robust, each with a dozen Fonderie Royale des Canons (Royal Cannon Foundry, or FRC) 47mm A/T guns, heavily supported by organic (24 Schneider Modèle (Mle.)13 105mm and Ehrhardt Mle.06 75mm field guns) and corps (36 Schneider Mle.17 155mm, Mle.13 105mm, and Cockerill Mle.32 120mm guns) artillery. However, the infantry lacked motor transport and the artillery was horse-drawn. The two cavalry divisions were more mobile, comprising eight motorcycle-mounted and two lorried regiments, with two regiments of (24 each) truck towed Mle.06 75mm field guns. The two ChA light divisions were largely bicycle-mounted, each supported by a motorized battalion of 12 Mle.34 75mm mountain howitzers.

Eschewing armour as 'an offensive weapon', the Belgian Army was slow to add tanks to its arsenal, eventually adding tiny detachments (a dozen each) of small T-13 'tank destroyers' (47mm A/T gun) to nine infantry divisions, with the two cavalry divisions including 18 of these plus an equal number of Vickers/FRC 4-ton machine gun-armed T-15 tankettes. One month before the invasion, 90 T-13s and T-15s were gathered into an ad hoc 'armoured brigade' and attached to the Groepering Keyaerts (K-Grp) in the Ardennes. Eight Renault ACG-1 (French AMC 35) 14.3-ton light tanks, also armed with 47mm cannon, formed the Cavalry Corps' Tank Squadron, which was held in reserve at Brussels.

The air arm – Aéronautique Militaire (AéM) – was organized into three regiments tailored to support army operations, but was almost completely composed of obsolete biplanes. 1ere Regiment d'Aéronautique (1ere RAé)

Military modernization, Belgian style: the Belgian cavalry enhanced its mobility through the extensive use of motorcycles (Sarolea Type 37 solo and an FN Type 12 sidecar motorcycle seen here) and acquired 211 small mechanized vehicles. In the background are two machine gun-armed T-15 tankettes, one T-13 B3 (turreted 47mm) 'tank destroyer', and a T-13 B1 tracked FRC 47mm (rearward facing) A/T gun. (Thomas Laemlein)

provided battlefield observation with six escadrilles (squadrons) containing 41 ancient Fairey Fox biplanes and 21 obsolescent Renard R.31s. The fighters were grouped in 2eme RAé and were a polyglot collection of 39 Gloster Gladiator and Fiat CR.42 Falco biplanes, 29 ancient Fox VI/VIII two-seat reconnaissance-fighter biplanes, and a single escadrille of 11 Hurricanes. The tactical bomber force (3eme RAé) consisted of 37 patently obsolete Fox biplanes and a single squadron of nine operational Fairey Battle monoplanes.

The Dutch

The Dutch were a peaceful people whose government invested very little in defence, and its Koninklijke Landmacht ('royal army') had not engaged in combat since 1830. Mobilized in August 1939, it fielded 114,000 men organized into nine divisions – eight infantry and one light (cyclist) – and two brigade groups. Additionally, there were 24 frontier battalions guarding the roads, railroads, and waterways entering the nation, and another 16 battalions positioned to slow the enemy's advance through inundations and bridge demolitions.

Lacking the robust ancillary elements needed for offensive operations (heavy weapons, assault guns, pioneers), Dutch infantry divisions were small – only 10,000 men – compared to the Germans' 17,000-man formation. The Veldleger was deficient in artillery, having only 310 outdated Krupp 75mm field pieces and 52 modern Bofors 105mm howitzers. While their A/T guns were modern Böhler 47mm weapons, only 386 were available. There were only 32 armoured cars and five ancient machine gun-armed Carden Loyd weapons carriers, precursors to the ubiquitous Vickers Universal Carrier.

The army's only mobile formation was the small Lichte Divisie, consisting of two bicyclist regiments, one motorcyclist battalion, and a small regiment of motorized 'horse artillery' (16 truck-towed 75mm field guns). (The Dutch use a variety of terms – brigades, regiments, halfregiments and battalions – to indicate battalion-size combat formation. For consistency, especially in relation to German or Allied units of similar strength, 'battalion' will be used throughout this work – except unit titles – to indicate these units.) While its on-road mobility was fairly fast, the 8,500-man unit lacked the hitting power needed to deal with mechanized units, and the staying power to engage the enemy for any appreciable duration.

The army's air arm, the Militaire Luchtvaart ('Military Aviation' or ML), consisted of two Luchtvaart regiments (LvRs – the 3e LvR being the training organization) with 126 operational aircraft. The 1e LvR provided the basis for the Air Defence Command (Commando Luchtverdediging), composed of four small squadrons, two flying 20 obsolete, single-engine Fokker D.21s and two with 23 modern, twin-engine G.1 Jachtkruisers. The 1e LvR's 'strategic group' was assigned directly to the High Command and had a squadron of nine obsolescent Fokker T.5 twin-engine bombers (Bombardeervliegtuig

The Dutch Army was almost exclusively an infantry organization, with some artillery and anti-tank support. Its only mobile formation was the bicycle-mounted Lichte Divisie ('Light Division'), seen here on manoeuvres along one of Holland's ubiquitous canals. (NIMH)

Afdeling or BomVA) and a reconnaissance squadron (Strategische Verkenningsvliegtuig Afdeling or StratVerVA) with ten obsolete C.10 biplanes.

The 2e Luchtvaart Regiment was assigned to the Veldleger and consisted of four squadron-sized 'groups' – one for each *legerkorps* ('army corps') – totalling 30 ancient Fokker C.5/C.10s and 15 light Koolhoven F.K.51 observation biplanes, plus one squadron of eight D.21s and another with 11 American-built Douglas DB-8/3N two-seat attack aircraft.

The Koninklijke Marine ('royal navy' or KM) was primarily organized to defend the expansive Netherlands East Indies (NEI). Consequently most of the fleet units were stationed in the NEI, leaving the old light cruiser *Sumatra*, destroyer *Jan van Galen*, five gunboats, and three coastal submarines as the main combat elements protecting the coast and the IJsselmeer. The Marine Luchtvaartdienst's ('naval air service' or MLD) only modern aircraft were seven twin-engine Fokker T.8W maritime reconnaissance floatplanes. The Korpsmariners' ('marine corps') operational unit was the battalion-size Rotterdam Garrison, comprising 450 men, almost half of which were still in training.

To defend against air attacks as well as airborne assaults, the Dutch Army purchased 355 first-rate anti-aircraft guns, including 155 excellent Oerlikon and Scotti 20mm pieces. Insufficient to provide a comprehensive defence, these were concentrated at the ML's airfields and other strategic points. (NIMH)

ORDERS OF BATTLE, 10 MAY 1940

GERMAN FORCES

HEERESGRUPPE B – GENERALOBERST FEDOR VON BOCK
Luftlandekorps (Luftwaffe) – Generalleutnant Kurt Student
7. Fliegerdivision – Generalleutnant Kurt Student
  FJR 1
  FJR 2 (-)
  Sturmabteilung 'Koch'
  Korpsführungskette   5 Do 17Ms
  Aufklärungsstaffel zbV.1
        3 Do 17Ms/4 Hs 126Bs
  KGzbV 1   208 Ju 52/3ms
  KGzbV 2   204 Ju 52/3ms
  17./KGrzbV 5
        48 Ju 52/3ms, 50 DFS 230As
  Sonderstaffel 'Schwilden'
        12 He 59C-2s
22. Infanterie-Division (Luftlande) –

Generalleutnant Hans Graf von Sponeck
  IR 16
  IR 47
  IR 65
  AR 22 (+)
AOK 6 – Generaloberst Walter von Reichenau
Army Reserve
  61. Infanterie-Division
  216. Infanterie-Division
  255. Infanterie-Division
I Armeekorps – Generalleutnant Hans-Kuno von Both
  1. Infanterie-Division – Generalmajor Philipp Kleffel
    IR 1
    IR 22
    IR 43
    AR 1

11. Infanterie-Division – Generalleutnant Herbert von Böckmann
  IR 2
  IR 23
  IR 44
  AR 11
223. Infanterie-Division – Generalleutnant Paul-Willi Körner
  IR 344
  IR 385
  IR 425
  AR 223
IV Armeekorps – General der Infanterie Viktor von Schwedler
  4. Panzer-Division – Generalleutnant Johann Joachim Stever
    PzR 35
    PzR 36

SR (mot.) 12
SR (mot.) 33
AR (mot.) 103
18. Infanterie-Division –
Generalleutnant Friedrich-Carl Cranz
   IR 30
   IR 51
   IR 54
   AR 18
35. Infanterie-Division –
Generalleutnant Hans Wolfgang
Reinhard
   IR 34
   IR 109
   IR 111
   AR 35
IX Armeekorps – General der Infanterie
Hermann Geyer
   19. Infanterie-Division – Generalmajor
   Otto von Knobelsdorff
      IR 59
      IR 73
      IR 74
      AR 19
   30. Infanterie-Division –
   Generalleutnant Kurt von Briesen
      IR 6
      IR 26
      IR 46
      AR 30
   56. Infanterie-Division – Generalmajor
   Karl Kriebel
      IR 171
      IR 192
      IR 234
      AR 156
XI Armeekorps – Generalleutnant
Joachim von Kortzfleisch
   7. Infanterie-Division –
   Generalleutnant Eccard Freiherr von
   Gablenz
      IR 19
      IR 61
      IR 62
      AR 7
   14. Infanterie-Division –
   Generalleutnant Peter Weyer
      IR 11
      IR 53
      IR 101
      AR 74

31. Infanterie-Division –
Generalleutnant Rudolf Kämpfe
   IR 12
   IR 17
   IR 82
   AR 31
XVI Armeekorps (mot.) – General der
Kavallerie Erich Hoepner
   3. Panzer-Division – Generalmajor
   Horst Stumpff
      PzR 5
      PzR 6
      SR (mot.) 3
      AR (mot.) 75
   20. Infanterie-Division (mot.) – General
   der Infanterie Mauritz von Wiktorin
      IR 76
      IR 80
      AR 20
XXVII Armeekorps – General der
Infanterie Alfred Wäger
   253. Infanterie-Division –
   Generalleutnant Fritz Kühne
      IR 453
      IR 464
      IR 473
      AR 253
   269. Infanterie-Division –
   Generalmajor Ernst-Eberhard Hell
      IR 469
      IR 489
      IR 490
      AR 269

**AOK 18 – General der Artillerie Georg
von Küchler**
Army Reserve
   XXXIX Korps HQ – Generalleutnant
   Rudolf Schmidt
   208. Infanterie-Division
   225. Infanterie-Division
X Armeekorps – Generalleutnant
Christian Hansen
   1. Kavallerie-Division – Generalmajor
   Kurt Feldt
      RR 1
      RR 2
      RR 22
      RAB 1
      RAB 2
   207. Infanterie-Division –
   Generalleutnant Carl von Tiedemann

      IR 322
      IR 368
      IR 374
      AR 207
      Attached: SS Standarte 'Der Führer'
   227. Infanterie-Division –
   Generalleutnant Friedrich Zickwolff
      IR 328
      IR 366
      IR 412
      AR 227
      Attached: SS Leibstandarte 'Adolf
      Hitler'
XXVI Armeekorps – Generalleutnant
Albert Wobig
   9. Panzer-Division – Generalleutnant
   Dr Alfred Ritter von Hubicki
      PzR 33
      SR (mot.) 10
      SR (mot.) 11
      AR (mot.) 102 (+)
      Aufkl-Rgt (mot.) 9
   254. Infanterie-Division –
   Generalleutnant Walter Behschnitt
      IR 454
      IR 474
      IR 484
      AR 254
   256. Infanterie-Division –
   Generalleutnant Gerhard Kauffmann
      IR 456
      IR 476
      IR 481
      AR 256
   SS Verfügungsdivision (mot.) –
   Gruppenführer Paul Hausser
      SS Standarte 'Deutschland'
      SS Standarte 'Germania'
      SS Artillerie Regiment

**LUFTWAFFE –
GENERALFELDMARSCHALL
HERMANN GÖRING**

(Note: numbers represent serviceable
aircraft strength on 10 May 1940)
**Luftflotte 2 – General der Flieger
Albert Kesselring**
Aufklärungsgruppe 122 (-)
        8 Ju 88As/17 He 111Hs
**Fliegerkorps z.b.V. – Generalmajor
Richard Putzier (HQ: Bremen)**

KG 4	59 He 111H/Ps	
	21 Ju 88As	
KG 54	90 He 111Ps	
IV.(St)/LG 1	37 Ju 87Bs	
Aufklärungsstaffel zbV.2		
	5 Do 17Ms/1 He 111Hs	

Fliegerkorps IV – General der Flieger Alfred Keller

KG 27	86 He 111Ps
KG 30	72 Ju 88As
LG 1	49 He 111Hs
	14 Ju 88As
1.(F)/121	8 He 111Hs/2 Ju 88As

Fliegerkorps VIII – Generalmajor Wolfram von Richthofen

StG 2	97 Ju 87Bs
StG 77	64 Ju 87Bs
II.(Schlact)/LG 2	38 Hs 123As
KG 77	83 Do 17Zs
JG 27	115 Bf 109Es
2(F)/123	10 Do 17Ps

Jagdfliegerführer 1 (Jafü 'Deutsche Bucht') – Oberstleutnant Carl Schumacher

JG 1	39 Bf 109Es
I.(J)/LG 2	32 Bf 109Es
II.(J)/Trägergruppe 186	35 Bf 109Es
IV.(N)/JG 2	30 Bf 109Ds

Jagdfliegerführer 2 – Generalmajor Hans von Döring (HQ: Dortmund)

JG 26	86 Bf 109Es
JG 51	147 Bf 109Es
ZG 1	48 Bf 110Cs
ZG 26	44 Bf 110Cs

Flakkorps II – Generalleutnant Otto Dessloch

III. FlaK-Bde
FlaK-Rgt. 6
FlaK-Rgt. 201
FlaK-Rgt. 202
FlaK-Rgt. 104

ALLIED FORCES

FRENCH ARMY – GÉNÉRAL D'ARMÉE MAURICE GAMELIN, COMMANDANT SUPRÊME DES ARMÉES ALLIÉES

Théâtre d'Opérations du Nord-Est – Général d'Armée Alphonse-Joseph Georges

GROUPE D'ARMÉES 1 – Général d'Armée Gaston H. G. Billotte

1ère Armée – Général Jean Georges Blanchard

    Commandant les Chars – GBC 514 and GBC 515

Corps de Cavalerie – Général René Prioux
  2e Division Légère Mécanique – Général de Brigade Gabriel Bougrain
    8e Cuirassiers
    13e Dragons
    29e Dragons
    1ère RDP
    71ère RATTT (+)
  3e Division Légère Mécanique – Général Jean-Léon-Albert Langlois
    1ère Cuirassiers
    2e Cuirassiers
    12e Cuirassiers
    11e RDP
    76e RATTT (+)
3e Corps d'Armée – General Benoît-Léon de La Laurencie
  6e GRCA
  603e RP
  105e RALH
  1ère Division d'Infanterie Motorisée –

Général Malivoire de Camas
  1ère RI
  43e RI
  110e RI
  15e RAD
  215e RALD
  7e GRDIm
2e Division d'Infanterie Nord Africaine – Général Pierre Dame
  11e RZ
  13e RTA
  22e RTA
  40e RANA
  240e RANLA
  92e GRDI
4e Corps d'Armée – Général Henri Aymes
  7e GRCA
  604e RP
  106e RALH
  15e Division d'Infanterie Motorisée – Général Alphonse Juin
    4e RI
    27e RI
    134e RI
    1ère RAD
    201ère RALD
    4e GRDIm
  1ère Division d'Infanterie Marocaine – Général Albert-Raymond Mellier
    1ère RTM
    2e RTM
    7e RTM
    64e RAA
    264e RALD

  80e GRDI
5e Corps d'Armée – Général Felix-René Altmayer
  3e GRCAm
  605e RP (+)
  104e RALA
  12e Division d'Infanterie Motorisée – Colonel Gaston Blanchon
    8e RZ
    106e RI
    150e RI
    25e RAD
    225e RALD
    3e GRDIm
  5e Division d'Infanterie Nord-Africaine – Général Augustin Agliany
    6e RTM
    14e RZ
    24e RTT
    25e RAD
    225e RALC
    95e GRDI
  101ère Division d'Infanterie de Forteresse – Général Louis Béjard
    84e RIF
    87e RIF
    148e RIF
    161ère RAP (-)
Reserve du Armée
  32e Division d'Infanterie – Colonel Savez
    7e RI
    122e RI
    143e RI

3e RAD

203e RALD

38e GRDI

7e Armée – Général d'Armée Henri H. Giraud

Commandant les Chars – GBC 510

Reconnaissance Groupement de Beauchesne

4e RDP (from 1ère DLM)

2e GRDIm (from 9e DIM)

12e GRDI (from 4e DI)

27e GRDIm (from 21re DI)

Reconnaissance Groupement Lestoquoi (attached to 1ère DLM)

2e GRCAm (from 1ère CA)

5e GRDIm (from 25e DIM)

1ère Corps d'Armée – Général Théodore Sciard

601ère RP, 101ère RALA

25e Division d'Infanterie Motorisée – Général Jean-Baptiste Molinié

38e RI

92e RI

121ère RI

16e RAD

216e RALD

16e Corps d'Armée – Général Alfred Fagalde

616e RP, 115e RALH

9e Division d'Infanterie Motorisée – Général Henri Didelet

13e RI

95e RI

131ère RI

30e RADT

230e RALDT

18e GRCA (from 16e CA)

Secteur Fortifié des Flandres – Général Eugène Barthélémy

272e Demi-Brigade d'Infanterie

21ère Centre d'Instruction Divisionnaire

I/161ère RAP (-)

Reserve du Armée

1ère Division Légère Mecanique – Général François Picard

4e Cuirassiers

6e Cuirassiers

18e Dragons

74e RATTT

21ère Division d'Infanterie – Général Félix Lanquetot

48e RI

65e RI

137e RI

35e RAD

255e RALD

6e Division d'Infanterie – Général Marcel Deslaurens

241ère RI

270e RI

271ère RI

50e RAD(+)

68e GRDI

68e Division d'Infanterie – Général Maurice Beaufrère

224re RI

225e RI

341ère RI

89e RAD

289e RALD (+)

59e GRDI

Armée de l'Air (AdA) – Général Joseph Vuillemin

Forces Aeriennes de Cooperation du Front Nord-Est – Général Marcel Têtu

Zone d'Operations Aériennes Nord – Général François d'Astier de La Vigerie (Note: numbers represent serviceable aircraft strength on 10 May 1940)

Fighters:

Groupement de Chasse No 23 – Général Jean Romatet

GC III/2	28 MS 406s
	Allocated to 1ère Armée
GC III/3	23 MS 406s
	Arrived 10 May

Groupement de Chasse No 25 – Colonel de Moussac

GC III/1	20 MS 406s
	Allocated to 7e Armée
GC I/4	26 H-75s
	Arrived 10 May
GC II/8	11 MB 152s
	Coastal air defence

Tactical Reconnaissance:

GR I/14	Potez 63-11
	Assigned to 1ère Armée
GR I/35	Potez 63-11
	Assigned to 7e Armèe

Aéronautique Navale:

F1C Flotille de Chasse

AC 1 and AC 2	24 Potez 631s
	Calais-Marck

F1A Flotilla du Béarn

AB 2	12 LN 401s
	Berck-sur-Mer
AB 3	12 Vought 156Fs
	Boulogne-Alprech

BRITISH FORCES

British Expeditionary Force (BEF) – General Lord Gort

I Corps – Lieutenant-General Michael Barker

27th and 140th Field Artillery Rgts

3rd and 5th Medium Rgts

52nd Light AA Rgt

1st Division – Major-General Harold Alexander

1st Guards Brigade

2nd Brigade

3rd Brigade

2nd, 19th, and 67th Field Artillery Rgts

21st A/T Rgt

2nd Division – Major-General Henry Loyd

4th Brigade

5th Brigade

6th Brigade

10th, 16th and 99th Field Artillery Rgts

13th A/T Rgt

48th (South Midland) Division – Major-General Andrew Thorne

143rd Brigade

144th Brigade

145th Brigade

18th, 25th, and 68th Field Artillery Rgts

53rd A/T Rgt

II Corps – Lieutenant-General Alan Brooke

60th and 88th Field Artillery Rgts

53rd and 59th Medium Rgts

53rd Light AA Rgt

3rd Division – Major-General Bernard Montgomery

7th Guards Brigade

8th Brigade

9th Brigade

7th, 33rd, and 76th Field Artillery Rgts

20th A/T Rgt

4th Division – Major-General Dudley

Johnson

  10th Brigade

  11th Brigade

  12th Brigade

  22nd, 30th, and 77th Field Artillery Rgts

  14th A/T Rgt

50th Division – Major-General Giffard Martel

  150th Brigade

  151st Brigade

  25th Brigade

  72nd and 74th Field Artillery Rgts

  65th A/T Rgt

III Corps – Lieutenant-General Ronald Adam

  3rd Rgt Royal Horse Artillery

  97th Field Artillery Rgt

  51st and 56th Medium Rgts

  54th Light AA Rgt

42nd (East Lancashire) Division – Major-General William Holmes

  125th Brigade

  126th Brigade

  127th Brigade

  52nd and 53rd Field Artillery Rgts

  56th A/T Rgt

44th (Home Counties) Division – Major-General Edmund Osborne

  131st Brigade

  132nd Brigade

  133rd Brigade

  57th, 58th, and 65th Field Artillery Rgts

  57th A/T Rgt

Line of Communications Troops

  12th (Eastern) Division – Major-General Roderic Petre

    35th Brigade

    36th Brigade

    37th Brigade

  23rd (Northumbrian) Division – Major-General Arthur Herbert

    69th Brigade

    70th Brigade

  46th (North Midland and West Riding) Division – Major-General Henry Curtis

    137th Brigade

    138th Brigade

    139th Brigade

General Headquarters (GHQ) Forces

  5th Division (BEF Reserve) – Major-

General Harold Franklyn

  13th Brigade

  17th Brigade

  9th, 91st, and 92nd Field Artillery Rgts

  52nd A/T Rgt

1st Tank Brigade

1st and 2nd Armoured Reconnaissance Brigades

1st, 2nd, and 4th AA Brigades

1st and 2nd Rgts, Royal Horse Artillery

Four medium field artillery regiments

Eight medium, three heavy and three super-heavy artillery regiments

Note: 51st (Highland) Division attached to French 3e Armée, behind the Maginot Line.

Royal Air Force

British Air Forces in France – Air Marshal Arthur Barratt

BEF Air Component – Air Vice Marshal Charles Blount

50 (Army Cooperation) Wing – Group Captain Churchman

4 Squadron	Lysanders
13 Squadron	Lysanders
16 Squadron	Lysanders

51 (Army Cooperation) Wing – Wing Commander Eccles

4 Squadron	Lysanders
13 Squadron	Lysanders
16 Squadron	Lysanders

60 (Fighter) Wing – Wing Commander Boret

85 Squadron	Hurricane Is
87 Squadron	Hurricane Is

61 (Fighter) Wing – Wing Commander Eccles

607 Squadron	Hurricane Is
615 Squadron	Gladiators – re-equipping with Hurricane Is

63 (Fighter) Wing – Wing Commander Finch (deployed 10 May 1940)

3 Squadron	Hurricane Is
79 Squadron	Hurricane Is

70 (Reconnaissance) Wing – Wing Commander Opie

18 Squadron	Blenheim Is and Vs
57 Squadron	Blenheim IVs

Ancillary: 81 (Communications) Squadron   Tiger Moths

BELGIAN FORCES

Armée Belge – King Léopold III

Ière Corps d'Armee – Lieutenant-général Vanderveken

  4eme Division d'Infanterie

    7eme Ligne Regiment

    11eme Ligne Regiment

    15eme Ligne Regiment

    8eme Artillerie Regiment

  7eme Division d'Infanterie

    18eme Ligne Regiment

    2eme Grenadiers Regiment

    2eme Carabiniers Regiment

    12eme Artillerie Regiment

IIeme Corps d'Armee – Lieutenant-général Michem

  6eme Division d'Infanterie

    9eme Ligne Regiment

    1ère Grenadiers Regiment

    1ère Carabiniers Regiment

    6eme Artillerie Regiment

  9eme Division d'Infanterie

    8eme Ligne Regiment

    16eme Ligne Regiment

    17eme Ligne Regiment

    4eme Artillerie Regiment

IIIeme Corps d'Armee – Lieutenant-général de Krahe

  2eme Division d'Infanterie

    5eme Ligne Regiment

    6eme Ligne Regiment

    28eme Ligne Regiment

    2eme Artillerie Regiment

  3eme Division d'Infanterie

    1ère Ligne Regiment

    12eme Ligne Regiment

    25eme Ligne Regiment

    3eme Artillerie Regiment

  Brigade Cycliste Frontiere

    1ère Cycliste Frontiere Regiment

    2eme Cycliste Frontiere Regiment

  1ère Lanciers Regiment – detached from 2eme Division de Cavalerie

  4eme Carabiniers Cyclistes Regiment – detached from 2eme Division de Cavalerie

  Regiment de Fortresse de Liège

IVeme Corps d'Armee – Lieutenant-général Bogaerts

  11eme Division d'Infanterie

    14eme Ligne Regiment

    20eme Ligne Regiment

29eme Ligne Regiment

9eme Artillerie Regiment

12eme Division d'Infanterie

2eme Ligne Regiment

22eme Ligne Regiment

23eme Ligne Regiment

7eme Artillerie Regiment

15eme Division d'Infanterie

31ere Ligne Regiment

42eme Ligne Regiment

43eme Ligne Regiment

23eme Artillerie Regiment

18eme Division d'Infanterie

39eme Ligne Regiment

3eme Grenadiers Regiment

3eme Carabiniers Regiment

26eme Artillerie Regiment

Veme Corps d'Armee – Lieutenant-général Vandenbergen

13eme Division d'Infanterie

32eme Ligne Regiment

33eme Ligne Regiment

34eme Ligne Regiment

21ère Artillerie Regiment

17eme Division d'Infanterie

7eme Chasseurs à Pied Regiment

8eme Chasseurs à Pied Regiment

9eme Chasseurs à Pied Regiment

25eme Artillerie Regiment

VIIeme Corps d'Armee – Lieutenant-général Deffontaine

2eme Division Chasseurs Ardennais

4eme Chasseurs Ardennais Regiment

5eme Chasseurs Ardennais Regiment

6eme Chasseurs Ardennais Regiment

8eme Division d'Infanterie

13eme Ligne Regiment

19eme Ligne Regiment

21ère Ligne Regiment

5eme Artillerie Regiment

Regiment de Forteresse de Namur

Corps de Cavalerie – Lieutenant-général de Neve de Roden

1ère Division d'Infanterie

3eme Ligne Regiment

4eme Ligne Regiment

24eme Ligne Regiment

1ère Artillerie Regiment

14eme Division d'Infanterie

35eme Ligne Regiment

36eme Ligne Regiment

38eme Ligne Regiment

22eme Artillerie Regiment

2eme Division de Cavalerie

1ère Chasseurs à Cheval Regiment

1ère Carabiniers Cyclistes Regiment

2eme Guides (cavalerie portes) Regiment

18eme Artillerie Regiment

Groepering-K – Lieutenant-général Kayerts

1ère Division de Cavalerie

2eme Chasseurs à cheval Regiment

2eme Carabiniers Cyclistes Regiment

1ère Guides (cavalerie portes) Regiment

2eme Lanciers Cyclistes Regiment

3eme Lanciers Cyclistes Regiment

17eme Artillerie Regiment

1ère Division Chasseurs Ardennais

1ère Chasseurs Ardennais Regiment

2eme Chasseurs Ardennais Regiment

3eme Chasseurs Ardennais Regiment

Ghent Garrison – 16eme Division d'Infanterie

37eme Ligne Regiment

41ère Ligne Regiment

44eme Ligne Regiment

24eme Artillerie Regiment

Reserve d'Armee:

VIeme Corps d'Armee – Lieutenant-général Vaerstraete

5eme Division d'Infanterie

1ère Chasseurs à Pied Regiment

2eme Chasseurs à Pied Regiment

4eme Chasseurs à Pied Regiment

11ère Artillerie Regiment

10eme Division d'Infanterie

3eme Chasseurs à Pied Regiment

5eme Chasseurs à Pied Regiment

6eme Chasseurs à Pied Regiment

10eme Artillerie Regiment

Escadron d'auto-blindees du Corps de Cavalerie

12 artillery regiments

Five frontier cyclists battalions

Two gendarmerie regiments

Defence Aerienne du Territoire – Lieutenant-général Duvivier

Aéronautique Militaire – Général-major Hiernaux

1ère Regiment d'Aéronautique – Colonel Foidart

Escadrille 1/I/1	10 Fairey Fox IIICs
Escadrille 3/II/1	12 Fairey Fox II/IIICs
Escadrille 5/III/1	10 Fairey Fox IIICs
Escadrille 7/IV/1	9 Fairey Fox VICs
Escadrille 9/V/1	11 Renard R.31s
Escadrille 11/VI/1	10 Renard R.31s

2eme Regiment d'Aéronautique – Colonel de Woelmont

Escadrille 1/I/2	15 Gloster Gladiators
Escadrille 2/I/2	11 Hawker Hurricanes
Escadrille 3/II/2	14 Fiat CR.42s
Escadrille 4/II/2	11 Fiat CR.42s
Escadrille 5/III/2	15 Fairey Fox VI/VIIIs
Escadrille 6/III/2	14 Fairey Fox VI/VIIIs

3eme Regiment d'Aéronautique – Colonel Hugon

Escadrille 1/I/3	14 Fairey Fox IIICs
Escadrille 3/I/3	14 Fairey Fox IIICs
Escadrille 5/III/3	9 Fairey Battles
Escadrille 7/III/3	9 Fairey Fox VICs

Defense Terrestre Contre Aeronefs (DTCA) – Général de brigade Frère

1ère Regiment d'DTCA

2eme Regiment d'DTCA

DUTCH FORCES

Koninklijke Landmacht – Generaal Henri G. Winkelman

Veldleger (Field Army) – Luitenant-Generaal Jan Baron van Voorst tot Voorst

Ie Legerkorps – (Army Reserve) – Generaal-Majoor Nicholas Carstens

1e Divisie

Regiment Jagers

Regiment Grenadiers

4e Regiment Infanterie

2e Regiment Artillerie

3e Divisie

1e Regiment Infanterie

9e Regiment Infanterie

12e Regiment Infanterie

6e Regiment Artillerie

3e Halfregiment Huzaren

10e Regiment Artillerie

IIe Legerkorps – Generaal-Majoor Jacob Herberts

2e Divisie

10e Regiment Infanterie

15e Regiment Infanterie

22e Regiment Infanterie

4e Regiment Artillerie

4e Divisie

8e Regiment Infanterie

11e Regiment Infanterie

19e Regiment Infanterie

8e Regiment Artillerie

4e Halfregiment Huzaren

12e Regiment Artillerie

IIIe Legerkorps – Generaal-Majoor Adrianus Nijnatten

5e Divisie

2e Regiment Infanterie (-)

13e Regiment Infanterie (-)

17e Regiment Infanterie (-)

3e Regiment Artillerie

6e Divisie

3e Regiment Infanterie (-)

6e Regiment Infanterie (-)

14e Regiment Infanterie (-)

7e Regiment Artillerie

Lichte Divisie

1e Regiment Wielrijders

2e Regiment Wielrijders

2e Regiment Huzaren Motorrijders

Korps Rijdende Artillerie

2e Halfregiment Huzaren

11e Regiment Artillerie

IVe Legerkorps – Generaal-Majoor Adrianus R. van der Bent

7e Divisie

7e Regiment Infanterie

18e Regiment Infanterie

20e Regiment Infanterie

1e Regiment Artillerie

8e Divisie

5e Regiment Infanterie

16e Regiment Infanterie

21e Regiment Infanterie

5e Regiment Artillerie

1e and 5e Halfregiments Huzaren

9e Regiment Artillerie

Vesting Holland (Fortress Holland) Troops – Luitenant-Generaal Jan van Andel

Grebbe Line

13e Regiment Artillerie

15e Regiment Artillerie

18e Regiment Artillerie

19e Regiment Artillerie

Peel Line (a.k.a. 'Peel Division')

27e Regiment Infanterie

30e Regiment Infanterie

Six battalions from IIIe Legerkorps infantry regiments

20e Regiment Artillerie

Defence between Meuse and Lek rivers

Independent Brigade Group A

44e Regiment Infanterie

46e Regiment Infanterie

16e Regiment Artillerie

Independent Brigade Group B

24e Regiment Infanterie

29e Regiment Infanterie

21e Regiment Artillerie

Frontier Troops

Eight infantry regiments

17 frontier battalions

Internal Security

11 infantry regiments

Five frontier battalions

1e Regiment Huzaren Motorrijders

14e Regiment Artillerie

22e Regiment Artillerie

23e Regiment Artillerie

Militaire Luchtvaart (Army Aviation) – Luitenant-Generaal Petrus Best

1e Luchtvaart Regiment

Ie Groep ('Strategischegroep')

Strategic Reconnaissance Squadron (StratVerVA)   10 C.10s

Bombardment Squadron (BomVA)

9 T.5s

IIe Groep ('Jachtgroep')

1. JaVA	11 D.21s
2. JaVA	9 D.21s
3. JaVA	11 G.1s
4. JaVA	12 G.1s

2e Luchtvaart Regiment

Ie Verkenningsgroep

5 C.5ds/C.10s/4 FK-51s

IIe Verkenningsgroep

7 C.5ds/5 FK-51s

IIIe Verkenningsgroep

7 C.5ds/3 FK-51s

IVe Verkenningsgroep

7 C.5ds/3 FK-51s

Jachtgroep:

1-V-2.LvR	8 Fokker D.21s
3-V-2.LvR	11 Douglas DB-8A/3Ns

3e Luchtvaart Regiment

Elementary Training School

Vlissingen

Advanced Training School

Haamstede

Operational Training School

De Vlijt, Texel Island

Koninklijke Marine – Vice-Admiraal Johannes Fürstner

Coastal Squadron

Light cruiser Sumatra

Destroyer Van Galen

Three coastal submarines

Two gunboats

Five torpedo boats

One MTB

Eight minelayers

One minesweeper

IJsselmeer Squadron

3 gunboats

1 torpedo boat

3 minesweepers

Marine Luchtdienst (naval aviation)

GVT 2 and 4   7 T.8Ws

Six other GVTs

25 reconnaissance floatplanes

Elementary Training School

De Kooy airfield

Floatplane Training School

De Mok, Texel Island

Korpsmariners (marine corps) – Kolonel von Frijtag Drabbe

Rotterdam Garrison

Den Helder Depot

THE CAMPAIGN

UNTERNEHMEN 'F'

The swine has gone off to the West Front … Let's hope that we'll meet again after the war.

Oberst Hans Oster, Abwehr Officer, to Majoor J. G. Sas, Dutch Military Attaché, 2130 hours, 9 May 1940

The Luftwaffe strikes Holland: 10 May

At 0245hrs Berlin time the first of some 500 Luftwaffe bombers – 30 He 111Ps of I. Gruppe/Kampfgeschwader 54 (I./KG 54) – roared into the night sky from Quakenbrück, Germany, and turned west. Taking off first, they had the furthest to go: they were to bomb airfields near Boulogne and Calais, hoping to knock out AdA fighters based there, so that they could return later and bomb the cities' port facilities without interference.

About an hour later (0345–0400hrs) 79 Heinkel 111s and Junkers 88s from Putzier's other bomber wing, KG 4 'General Wever', took off from airfields around Bremen. In the pre-dawn darkness they headed out over the North Sea and turned to parallel the Dutch coast approximately 15 to 20 miles (24–30km) offshore. Guided by Dutch lightships, they flew in a long train-like procession until each *Gruppe* was abeam its assigned target. Nearly simultaneously, at 0530hrs they all turned inland and approached their target airfields from the west.

Consistent with their doctrine, the Luftwaffe launched the offensive with massive bombing strikes against Armée de l'Air, BEF (AC), Belgian, and Dutch airfields. Luftflotte 2 was imminently successful, destroying half the Dutch air force, decimating the Belgian air arm, and eliminating several French AdA and Aéronavale units. (IWM HU4991)

The Luftwaffe initial airfield attacks and air assaults, 10 May 1940.

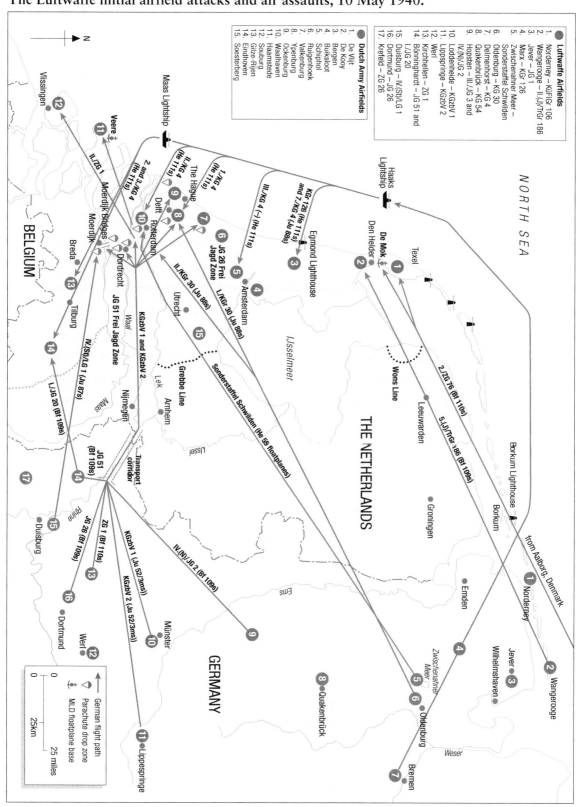

LEFT
Three squadrons of obsolete, fixed-gear, mixed construction Fokker D.21s scrambled to shoot down three Ju 88As, but were overwhelmed by the larger numbers of superior Messerschmitts, losing eight in aerial combat during the first day of the invasion. (Thijs Postma)

RIGHT
Air raid! The large Fokker G.1 Jachtkruiser was difficult to conceal in the flat, open Dutch countryside – of 23 on hand, eight were destroyed and nine damaged in the opening Luftwaffe air attacks. Some of the survivors got airborne to shoot down five He 111s and one Bf 109D. (Johann Schuurmann)

The Luftwaffe's second wave – 25 Ju 88s from KG 30 – departed from Oldenburg at 0430hrs to bomb Dutch AA batteries around the paratroopers' primary drop zones (DZs) at Ypenburg and Waalhaven. I./KG 30 headed straight for The Hague, while II./KG 30 winged towards Rotterdam.

Timing their flight across the Netherlands to reach the target areas simultaneously with the bombers' arrivals were large formations of Messerschmitt fighters sweeping deep into Holland by following the wide, wandering ribbon of the Waal River. Leading the way were two squadrons (10. and 12.(N)/JG 2) of Bf 109D night fighters – the only Luftwaffe fighter pilots trained to take off in the dark – arriving in the target areas at 0520hrs. Following them, two squadrons of the longer-ranged Bf 110 *Zerstörer* ('destroyer') from ZG 1 angled north-west to cover the three target airfields around The Hague while two others continued west to attack the ML's training bases at Haamstede and Souburg. Behind these came the Bf 109E day fighters, JG 26 covering the Amsterdam area and JG 51 patrolling the Rotterdam region.

The initial blows were delivered by Oberst Martin Fiebig's KG 4. 1. Staffel (eight He 111Hs) struck Ypenburg airfield, paving the way for Gruppe Nord's attempted *coup de main*. Beginning at 0525hrs eight Fokker D.21s and 11 Douglas DB-8As (the latter flying in the two-seat fighter role) scrambled to find themselves smothered by 22 *Zerstörer* (I./ZG 1). Almost immediately three D.21s and six DB-8As were shot down.

The key to the German airborne invasion was Waalhaven airfield and it was the target for II./KG 4 (28 He 111Ps), led by Fiebig and his *Geschwaderführungskette* ('wing leader flight'). Alerted by the noise of the approaching bombers, 3e Jacht Vliegtuig Afdeling ('3rd Fighter Aircraft Unit' or 3e JaVA) scrambled eight Fokker G.1s into the air and quickly shot down five He 111s, including Fiebig's, who survived to become a prisoner of war (POW) for the duration of the five-day campaign. However, only one G.1 escaped destruction. Three other G.1s, Waalhaven's hangars, buildings, perimeter defences, and the Koolhoven aircraft factory were destroyed by the rain of 110 lb (50kg) bombs.

Fiebig's third *Gruppe* (18 He 111Ps and six Ju 88As) attacked Schiphol airfield, where nine D.21s (2e JaVA) scrambled as the German bombers approached. Eight T.5s (BomVA) took off amid the bomb explosions that wrecked five others, the bombers establishing three combat air patrol (CAP) orbits – and soon used their Solothurn 20mm nose cannon to shoot down two Ju 52/3m transports (from 3./KGrzbV 9) – before dispersing to various Dutch airfields.

In its attack on Bergen airfield, five Ju 88A-5s from 7./KG 4 were assisted by 11 He 111Hs from Kampfgruppe 126 (KGr 126). The Junkers dive-bombed the new airfield's hangars from 9,844ft (3,000m) followed by the Heinkels, which plastered the parking ramps, hangars, and other buildings with bombs from 984ft (300m) altitude. Because of the moist, soft condition of the airfield, 4e JaVA's twelve serviceable G.1s were parked wingtip to wingtip on the concrete apron; three were destroyed and all but one were damaged in the attack.

The air battles did not always go the Luftwaffe's way. At De Kooy eight Bf 109Es were engaged by nine D.21s in a dogfight directly over the field. The slower, more nimble Fokkers shot down two 'Emils', one (seen here) 'bellying in' on the airfield. (Thijs Postma)

Defending the Dutch Navy's main fleet base of Den Helder, 1e JaVA was stationed at nearby De Kooy naval airfield. Learning of the Luftwaffe attacks on Waalhaven, the squadron scrambled its eleven D.21s and headed south to intercept enemy bombers. After a fruitless patrol, nine returned for refuelling just as eight Bf 109Es (from II.(Jacht)/Trägergruppe 186) arrived and began strafing, destroying one Fokker on its landing roll. In the swirling dogfight that ensued the nimble D.21s easily out-turned the faster Messerschmitts and shot down two of them. However, all the Dutch fighters were damaged in the ten-minute mêlée. Subsequent strafing raids found the airfield undefended and three more D.21s were destroyed on the ground.

Meanwhile Putzier's other bomber wing, Oberst Walter Lackner's KG 54, the *Totenkopf Geschwader* ('Death Head's Wing'), split into its three groups and struck Boulogne-Alprecht (where they wiped out the 12 Vought V-156F dive bombers of the French Aéronavale's escadrille AB 3), Calais-Marck, and Antwerp-Deurne.

In the first hour the Luftwaffe's decisive tactical superiority decimated the ML's combat force; only two serviceable G.1 and ten D.21 fighters, five T.5 bombers and ten C.10 reconnaissance biplanes remained. Despite overwhelming odds, the Dutch aircrews fought courageously and, according to German records, destroyed eight bombers (five He 111s and three Ju 88s), two Dornier reconnaissance aircraft, and five Bf 109s, as well as eight of the now-arriving Ju 52/3m transports.

Gruppe Nord – *the* coup de main

Only five minutes after the last 'flak suppression' Ju 88As (KG 30) headed back to Oldenburg to refuel and rearm, the first wave of the air assault forces approached from the east. This was a stream of 197 Ju 52/3m transports (primarily Oberst Friedrich-Wilhelm Morzik's KGzbV 1) lumbering along in 'javelin formation of groups', the first of which crossed the Dutch frontier, about halfway between Nijmegen and Arnhem, at 0530hrs and descended to 'hedge-hopping altitude' to follow the Waal River to a point east of Rotterdam. There IV. Gruppe angled off north-west towards The Hague while the following three *Gruppen* fanned out west and south-west. Arriving over their DZs nearly simultaneously, just before 0630hrs, the huge formations of Junkers Ju 52/3m climbed to 394ft (120m) altitude and began disgorging 'sticks' of paratroopers.

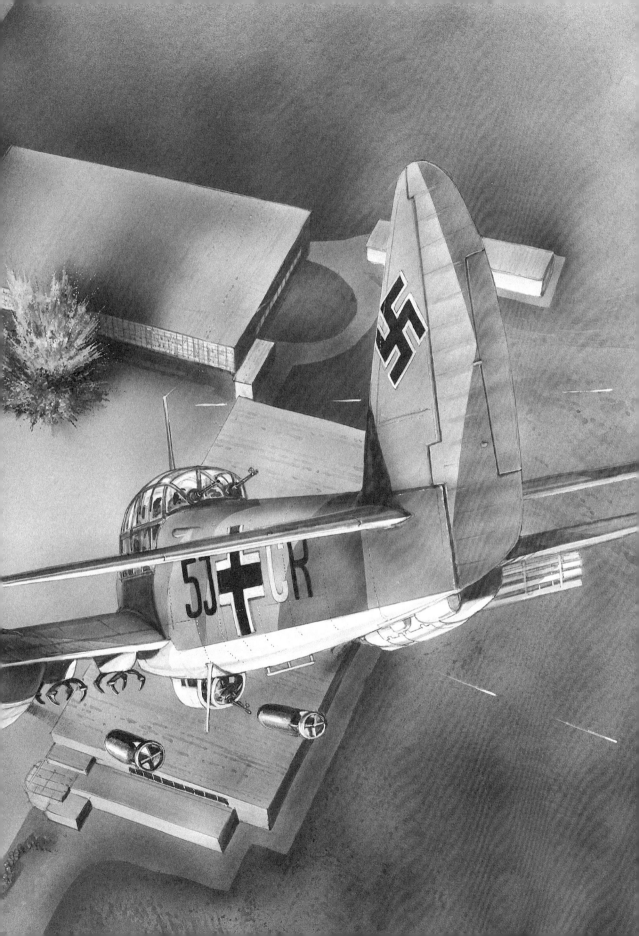

THE LUFTWAFFE STRIKES: BERGEN AIRFIELD, 0520HRS, 10 MAY 1940 (PP. 38–39)

Delayed due to a pre-dawn take-off accident that destroyed one aircraft (5J+HR) and killed its four-man crew, the remaining five Ju 88 A-5s of 7./KG 4 arrived at the *Kampfgeschwader*'s 'coast out point' near Emden late. It was essential that the Junkers, operating in the dive-bomber mode, attacked prior to the arrival of the level bombers (eleven He 111 H-2s from KGr 126), so Staffelkapitän Hauptmann Erich Blödorn led his small formation across the Dutch provinces of Groningen and Friesland to approach Bergen airfield from the north-east, while the Heinkels, having rounded the Dutch coast, came in from the North Sea.

Arriving overhead early at 0540hrs, with the sunrise just beginning in the east, from 9,844ft (3,000m) Blödorn tipped his Junkers over on one wing and went hurtling down towards his target: the twelve Fokker G.1s of 4e Jachtvliegtuig Afdeling (4e JaVA) arranged in three neat rows on the newly completed Platform 3. Because the new airfield's grass surface was still moist and soft, the heavy twin-engine Jachtkruisers ('fighter-cruisers') had to be parked on the concrete platform while the much lighter C.10 biplanes of the Strategische Verkenningsvliegtuig Afdeling ('strategic reconnaissance squadron', StratVerVA) were dispersed around the airfield's perimeter.

Blödorn **(1)** planted his two SC 500 1,102 lb bombs in front of Hangar 6 **(2)**, destroying one G.1 (#333) and damaging the ones around it. His wingmen **(3)** bombed hangars 5 and 6, destroying two more G.1s (#313 and #317) in the former. The KGr 126 Heinkels littered the hangars and platforms with smaller SC 50 bombs, ensuring that the buildings were destroyed and seven

G.1s were badly damaged, two of them (#301 and #332) beyond repair. Alerted by a telephone call from the Air Defence Command HQ five minutes before, the three G.1s of the '*alarm patrouille*' on the front row (G.1s #321, #304 and #331) started engines as the Ju 88s began their attacks, but only one Jachtkruiser **(4)** was able to scramble. However, 1e Luitenant-vlieger Johan W. Thijssen and gunner Sergeant K. Vermaat could not catch the raiders.

While two anti-aircraft (AA) batteries provided defence to the east and north-west with three Vickers 75mm and three Bofors 40mm guns, the only AA weapons on the field were two 7.92mm Spandau M.25 machine guns in positions atop and at the base of the control tower **(5)**. These slightly damaged three He 111s as they made their bomb runs.

While the StratVerVA survived relatively unscathed, having lost only two Fokker C.10s in Hangar 2, and began bombing operations against the German air assaults forces at Valkenburg, Waalhaven, and Moerdijk, the decimated 4e JaVA became the sole surviving G.1 unit, receiving one Jachtkruiser from Waalhaven (#315 from 3e JaVA) and another (#303) from the Fokker repair facility at Schiphol. During the next four days, despite having repaired five 4e JaVA machines, Bergen was never able to launch more than two or three fighters on a few ground attack and escort missions. Because it was a prime target, Bergen was attacked again that afternoon and several times during the next three days, eventually forcing G.1 operations to shift to Schiphol and the StratVerVA to Ruigenhoek.

The primary landing zone (LZ) for Gruppe Nord was Ypenburg airfield, where I./KG 30 had achieved little against the two Oerlikon 20mm cannon and 15 Spandau 7.92mm AA machine guns (MGs). Opening a devastating barrage against the 40 approaching Junkers (IV./KGzbV 1), the fierce flak shot down four transports, shattered the formations, and scattered 435 *Fallschirmjäger* (I./FJR 2 minus 3. Kompanie) across a 3-square mile (7.5km^2) area around the aerodrome, most of them landing to the south.

Ypenburg was defended by two companies of III Bataljon-Regiment Grenadiers (III-RGr), which were initially panicked by the aerial bombardment, but recovered to mount a stubborn resistance. The bombing disabled half of the six Landsverk L181/M.36 armoured cars (1e Esk Paw), but barely affected the AA batteries. The latter opened fire again at 0711hrs against the first wave of assault transports – 36 Ju 52/3ms (KGrzbV 12) carrying 429 men of II./IR 65 – shooting down 13, many of them crashing on the airfield, and forcing the others to divert elsewhere, ten landing on The Hague–Rotterdam motorway and seven others flying to Valkenburg.

West of the airfield the *Fallschirmjäger* were still battling the grenadiers when the second wave arrived – 40 Ju 52/3ms (KGrzbV 9) bringing in General Sponeck and 508 infantrymen, including the 22. Infanterie-Division staff, signals, pioneers, and motorcyclists. Six Junkers were shot down on finals and the rest scattered, 18 landing along The Hague–Rotterdam motorway, while 12 others, including the 3./KGrzbV 9 transport carrying Sponeck, diverted to Ockenburg.

Midmorning Oberst Georg Friemel, commanding IR 65, took charge of the operation, the 785 paratroopers and air assault infantrymen soon overrunning the Dutch defenders and capturing all but the north corner of the airfield. With 17 crashed transports burning on the landing grounds and the ground battle still ongoing, the third wave – 26 Ju 52/3ms (IV./KGzbV 1 on their second trip) attempting to bring in two infantry companies (I./IR 65) – diverted elsewhere, most of them landing at Waalhaven.

To the north, Valkenburg was a new ML air base and, like Bergen, the fresh sod of its landing grounds was still very soft. Consequently, it was not yet used by the ML, had no AA units and only two companies from III-4e RI guarding it. In fact, its main defence was that it blended well with the surrounding polder farms, this feature causing the Ju 52/3m pilots (4./KGrzvV 172) to miss the DZ entirely, depositing 61 *Fallschirmjäger* (two platoons from 6./FJR 2) on the beaches either side of the aerodrome at 0625hrs.

The paratroopers had only 25 minutes to organize their approach to the airfield before the first of 53 Junkers (KGrzbV 11) arrived to deliver 783 infantrymen of III./IR 47. One transport was shot down by the defenders' MG platoon and two diverted elsewhere – the other 50 landed safely, only to sink to their bellies in the marshy ground. These were followed ten minutes later by seven transports diverting from Ypenburg – that also became trapped – delivering 88 more troops. With the airfield congested with 57 wrecked transports, further landings were impossible.

The classic image of the German paratrooper assault. Taken by Dutch photographer Henk Lamme from his home's rooftop, a *Fallschirmjäger* platoon of I./FJR 2 are seen descending between Ypenburg airfield and the southern suburbs of The Hague. (NIMH)

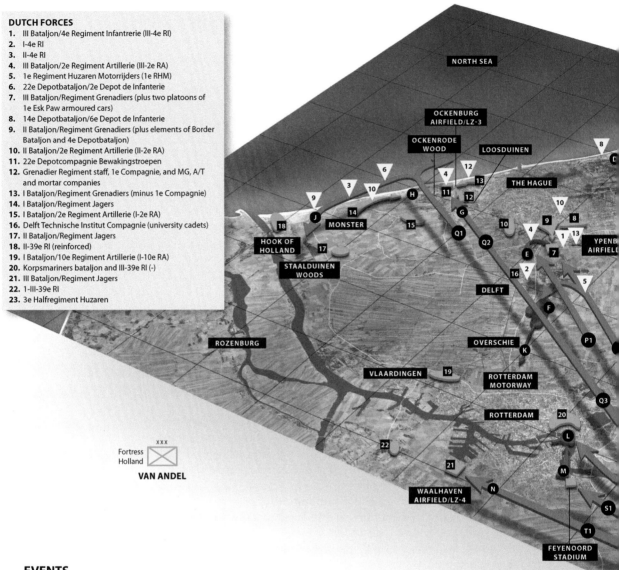

DUTCH FORCES

1. III Bataljon/4e Regiment Infanterrie (III-4e RI)
2. I-4e RI
3. II-4e RI
4. III Bataljon/2e Regiment Artillerie (III-2e RA)
5. 1e Regiment Huzaren Motorrijders (1e RHM)
6. 22e Depotbataljon/2e Depot de Infanterie
7. III Bataljon/Regiment Grenadiers (plus two platoons of 1e Esk Paw armoured cars)
8. 14e Depotbataljon/6e Depot de Infanterie
9. II Bataljon/Regiment Grenadiers (plus elements of Border Bataljon and 4e Depotbataljon)
10. II Bataljon/2e Regiment Artillerie (II-2e RA)
11. 22e Depotcompagnie Bewakingstroepen
12. Grenadier Regiment staff, 1e Compagnie, and MG, A/T and mortar companies
13. I Bataljon/Regiment Grenadiers (minus 1e Compagnie)
14. I Bataljon/Regiment Jagers
15. I Bataljon/2e Regiment Artillerie (I-2e RA)
16. Delft Technische Institut Compagnie (university cadets)
17. II Bataljon/Regiment Jagers
18. II-39e RI (reinforced)
19. I Bataljon/10e Regiment Artillerie (I-10e RA)
20. Korpsmariners bataljon and III-39e RI (-)
21. III Bataljon/Regiment Jagers
22. 1-III-39e RI
23. 3e Halfregiment Huzaren

EVENTS

1. 0628hrs: LZ-2 – disrupted by intense AA fire, IV./KGzbV 1 scatters I./FJR 2 in five groups, mostly to the south and west of Ypenburg.

2. 0630hrs: Delft – three Ju 52/3ms from 4./KGrzbV 172 drop one platoon of 6./FJR 2 south of Delft to secure section of Delft–Rotterdam motorway as an emergency landing strip. 'Gruppe Gunkelmann' annihilated by local Dutch recruits and university cadets.

3. 0635hrs: LZ-1 – seven Ju 52/3ms (two others shot down by T.5s) from 4./KGrzbV 172 overshoot DZ and drop half of 6./FJR 2 on beaches west of Valkenburg.

LZ-3 – 12 Ju 52/3ms (one other shot down by AA) from 16./KGrzbV 1 overshoot DZ and drop one platoon of 3./FJR 2 on beach south-west of Ockenburg, and another on Hook of Holland. Others fly north and drop the rest of 3./FJR 2 on beach west of Valkenburg.

4. 0700–0720hrs: LZ-1 – KGrzbV 11 lands III./IR 47 on Valkenburg, defeating defenders and securing the airfield, Oude Rijn bridges, and Leiden–The Hague motorway.

LZ-2 – KGrzbV 12 (minus) is repulsed with severe losses; ten Ju 52/3ms land elements of 6. and 8./IR 65 on The Hague–Rotterdam motorway south-east of Delft. Two hours later I./FJR 2 and II./IR 65 complete the capture of Ypenburg airfield.

LZ-3 – 3./KGrzbV 12 lands 5./IR 65 on Ockenburg, securing the airfield.

5. 0745hrs: LZ-3 – 1./KGrzbV 9 delivers Radf-Schw 2/AR 22 (two platoons).

LZ-2 – KGrzbV 9 (minus) driven off with heavy losses, 23 Ju 52/3ms land south-east of Delft, delivering 22. Inf-Div staff, signals, pioneers and 13./IR 47. Joining survivors of 6. and 8./IR 65, this force advances north, helping paratroopers capture Ypenburg airfield.

6. 0835–0842hrs: LZ-3 – ten Ju 52/3ms from 3./KGrzbV 9 diverting from Ypenburg land Gen Sponeck and 22. Inf-Div staff onto beaches and fields south-west of Ockenburg.

7. 0940hrs: LZ-1 – 1e RHM drives elements of III./IR 47 off the Leiden–The Hague motorway and back to Valkenburg airfield.

8. 1105–1135hrs: LZ-1 – 16 Ju 52/3ms from I./KGzbV 1 land 236 infantry of II./IR 47 on beaches west of Valkenburg, augmenting 60 paratroopers from 3./FJR 2 dropped in error near Katwijk.

9. 1140–1300hrs: Hook of Holland – ten Ju 52/3ms diverting from Ypenburg land parts of three companies of IR 65; 89 men withdraw into Staalduinen Wood, forming 'Gruppe Martin.'

10. 1240hrs: LZ-3 – after repulsing German attempts to enter The Hague and to capture Loosduinen, supported by I-2e RA, I-Grenadiers attack Ockenburg airfield and I-Jagers attack Ockenrode Wood.

LZ-2 – supported by II-2e RA, II-Grenadiers (reinforced) attack towards Ypenburg airfield.

11. 1400hrs: LZ-1 – two battalions of 4e RI, supported by III-2e RA, attack the north-west side of Valkenburg airfield, driving III./IR 47 into Valkenburg village.

12. 1600hrs: LZ-3 – Ockenburg airfield is recaptured; 'Gruppe Sponeck' concentrates 360 survivors in Ockenrode Wood.

13. 1630hrs: LZ-2 – Ypenburg airfield is recaptured; 1,295 survivors of 'Gruppe Friemel' are captured; 200 survivors form 'Gruppe Wischhusen' and escape to the south-east.

14. 1900hrs: LZ-1 – Valkenburg airfield is recaptured.

Fortress Holland
XXX
VAN ANDEL

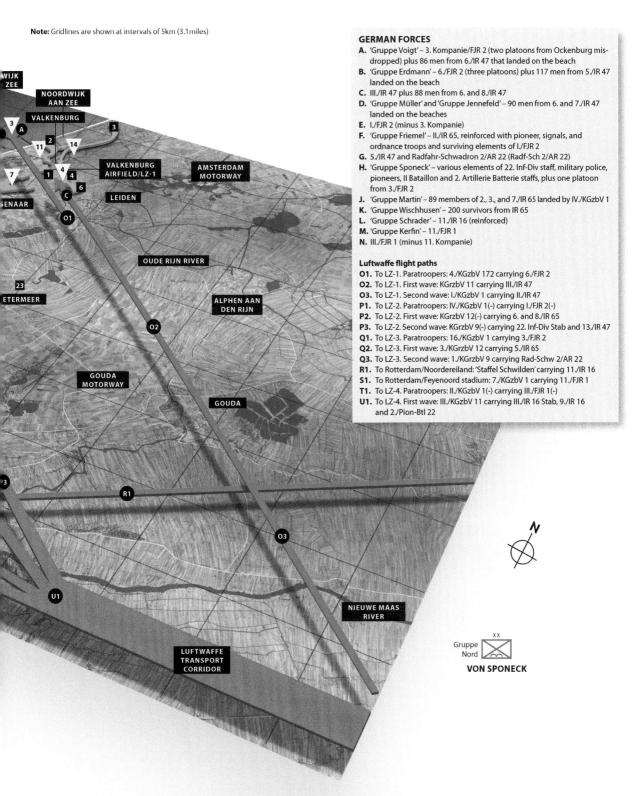

Note: Gridlines are shown at intervals of 5km (3.1miles)

GERMAN FORCES

A. 'Gruppe Voigt' – 3. Kompanie/FJR 2 (two platoons from Ockenburg mis-dropped) plus 86 men from 6./IR 47 that landed on the beach
B. 'Gruppe Erdmann' – 6./FJR 2 (three platoons) plus 117 men from 5./IR 47 landed on the beach
C. III./IR 47 plus 88 men from 6. and 8./IR 47
D. 'Gruppe Müller' and 'Gruppe Jennefeld' – 90 men from 6. and 7./IR 47 landed on the beaches
E. I./FJR 2 (minus 3. Kompanie)
F. 'Gruppe Friemel' – II./IR 65, reinforced with pioneer, signals, and ordnance troops and surviving elements of I./FJR 2
G. 5./IR 47 and Radfahr-Schwadron 2/AR 22 (Radf-Sch 2/AR 22)
H. 'Gruppe Sponeck' – various elements of 22. Inf-Div staff, military police, pioneers, II Bataillon and 2. Artillerie Batterie staffs, plus one platoon from 3./FJR 2
J. 'Gruppe Martin' – 89 members of 2., 3., and 7./IR 65 landed by IV./KGzbV 1
K. 'Gruppe Wischhusen' – 200 survivors from IR 65
L. 'Gruppe Schrader' – 11./IR 16 (reinforced)
M. 'Gruppe Kerfin' – 11./FJR 1
N. III./FJR 1 (minus 11. Kompanie)

Luftwaffe flight paths

O1. To LZ-1. Paratroopers: 4./KGzbV 172 carrying 6./FJR 2
O2. To LZ-1. First wave: KGrzbV 11 carrying III./IR 47
O3. To LZ-1. Second wave: I./KGzbV 1 carrying II./IR 47
P1. To LZ-2. Paratroopers: IV./KGzbV 1(-) carrying I./FJR 2(-)
P2. To LZ-2. First wave: KGzbV 12(-) carrying 6. and 8./IR 65
P3. To LZ-2. Second wave: KGrzbV 9(-) carrying 22. Inf-Div Stab and 13./IR 47
Q1. To LZ-3. Paratroopers: 16./KGzbV 1 carrying 3./FJR 2
Q2. To LZ-3. First wave: 3./KGrzbV 12 carrying 5./IR 65
Q3. To LZ-3. Second wave: 1./KGrzbV 9 carrying Rad-Schw 2/AR 22
R1. To Rotterdam/Noordereiland: 'Staffel Schwilden' carrying 11./IR 16
S1. To Rotterdam/Feyenoord stadium: 7./KGzbV 1 carrying 11./FJR 1
T1. To LZ-4. Paratroopers: II./KGzbV 1(-) carrying III./FJR 1(-)
U1. To LZ-4. First wave: III./KGzbV 11 carrying III./IR 16 Stab, 9./IR 16 and 2./Pion-Btl 22

Gruppe Nord

VON SPONECK

THE AIRBORNE *COUP DE MAIN* ATTEMPT AGAINST THE HAGUE, 10 MAY 1940

The German Gruppe Nord conducts airborne assaults on three airfields around The Hague (Valkenburg, Ypenburg, and Ockenburg). However, Dutch counter-attacks manage to recapture the airfields.

The Luftwaffe transport pilots assaulting the unfinished Valkenburg airfield – 50 Ju 52/3ms of KGrzbV 11 – were surprised to find that the airfield's landing surface was still a soft and soggy polder, and the heavily laden transports promptly sank up to their bellies. (Johann Schuurmann)

But the size of the German ground force was now considerable, the 857 invaders driving off the defenders, consolidating their hold on the airfield, securing their rear (north) flank, and starting an advance southwards towards The Hague. Deploying quickly from Wassenaar to block them was the battalion-size 1e Regiment Huzaren Motorrijders (1st Hussar Motorcycle Regiment) with one company of motorcycle-mounted cavalry and a truck-borne heavy weapons company with four A/T guns. After the initial clash the Germans withdrew into a defensive perimeter around the airfield and were soon under attack from the north by two other battalions from 4e RI.

At 1010hrs, as the Dutch infantry moved into position, the ML attacked Valkenburg airfield with five ancient C.5d observation aircraft (IIIe Verkenningsgroep) scattering 20 small 55 lb (25kg) bombs amongst the stranded transports. As soon as the Fokkers egressed, eight 12.5cm howitzers (III-2e RA) started shelling the airfield. The bombardments destroyed 55 Junkers, setting many aflame, and drove most of the Germans off the aerodrome and into Valkenburg village. Beginning at 1345hrs the Dutch ground attack eventually recaptured the airfield and later surrounded the village, which became the final redoubt of the 670 survivors of the air assault.

The third LZ, Ockenburg, was a complex of sports fields that the ML had acquired as a makeshift aircraft storage depot. Garrisoned by the 96-man 22e Depotcompagnie Bewakingstroepen (22nd Depot Company of Guard Troops), the field had no defensive positions or AA weapons; but it, too, was difficult to spot from the air. Most of the Ju 52/3m pilots (16./KGzbV 1) missed it entirely, only 40 of the 148 *Fallschirmjäger* (3./FJR 2) landing near the airfield. Thirty minutes later the first air assault wave – 17 Junkers (3./KGrzbV 12) with 221 troops (mostly 5./IR 65) – landed, the infantrymen engaging the lightly armed depot troops in a fierce fire-fight. The second wave arrived 45 minutes afterwards, ten transports (1./KGrzbV 9) delivering 121 bicycle reconnaissance troops (Radf-Schw 2./AR 22). The small airfield became so crowded with transports that ten more Junkers diverting from Ypenburg, including the one bearing Sponeck, had to land on nearby beaches, polders, or meadows.

Around 0930hrs, the more heavily armed Luftlande infantry finally overcame the depot's defenders, killing 28 and capturing 50 more, but the delay was sufficient to allow hasty but effective Dutch responses. During the battle the ML attacked with four T.5 bombers, dropping four 220 lb (100kg) and 16 110 lb (50kg) bombs, destroying six Ju 52/3ms. Patrolling Bf 110Cs (1./ZG 1) shot down one of the bombers. Due to the carnage and smoke the third wave – 12 Junkers (16./KGzbV 1) bearing 7./IR 65 – diverted elsewhere, ten landing safely at Waalhaven.

Unknown to the Germans, the nearby town of Loosduinen was home to the Grenadiers' HQ and its mortar, MG, and A/T companies, along with a reservist battery of ancient 5.7cm field guns. These deployed to face the attackers as they attempted to enter the town and, joined by a grenadier infantry company (1-I-RGr), they repulsed the invaders. The rest of the Grenadiers' I Bataljon deployed in a wooded park along the south edge of The Hague and at midday the grenadiers launched a coordinated counter-attack supported by a dozen 7.5cm guns (I-2e RA) whose bombardment destroyed another dozen Junkers on the airfield. Advancing from Loosduinen and The Hague, the grenadiers overran the German outer defences and soon reclaimed the airfield, capturing 179 Luftlande troops and driving the 360 survivors into the woods to the south.

The initially successful air assault on Ockenburg depot airfield turned sour once the Dutch Army reacted, its artillery pounding the Ju 52/3ms, effectively blocking the field for any reinforcements. (Bundesarchiv Bild 141-0460)

Meanwhile at Ypenburg, Friemel's infantry advanced to the south-east edge of The Hague. Here, too, the Dutch reacted quickly, sending various 'depot companies' to stop the invaders and, surprisingly, the untrained recruits drove the Germans back towards the airfield. At midday, II-RGr, reinforced with one depot company, organized a coordinated counter-attack supported by a dozen 7.5cm guns (II-2e RA) that proceeded slowly against stubborn resistance. Four hours later, just as the Dutch were beginning to retake the airfield, an incoming RAF attack caused a halt. At 1650hrs nine Bristol Blenheim IV light bombers (40 Sqn) attacked, adding to the savage devastation, losing three bombers to intercepting Bf 110C₃ (I./ZG 1) but enabling the final assault to reclaim the base.

In the mopping up operations that followed, the Dutch captured 1,295 German troops – including Friemel and the commanders of I./FJR 2 and KGrzbV 12 – but the destruction of the airfield prevented its use for three days. Some 200 survivors, south of Delft, withdrew into the small town of Overschie, just north of Rotterdam, hoping to be saved by the arrival of the ground forces.

His *coup de main* defeated, General Sponeck joined his troops in digging into defensive positions in the nearby Ockenburgse Bos (Ockenburg Woods). (Ryan Noppen)

Realizing that the initial objectives of the assault were beyond reach, Kesselring terminated the airborne assault and ordered the scattered units to fall back towards the bridgehead in Rotterdam. Some 3,550 of Sponeck's 6,500 Gruppe Nord troops had landed around the Dutch capital and the 1,650 survivors could only withdraw into neighbouring villages and forests, and hunker down to await relief by the approaching panzers.

'As far as we can ascertain,' Kesselring reported to Göring, '22. Luftlande Division operations … are near failure due to strong ground defence and enemy AA artillery.'

Gruppe Nord parachute and air assault assignments, 10 May 1940

Land time CEST	Transport unit	No. of aircraft	Troops aboard	Results
Ypenburg (Landing Zone 2)				
0628	IV./KGzbV 1 (minus 16.Staffel)	40	I./FJR 2 (minus 3. Company)	Paratroop drop on Ypenburg airfield; 5 Ju 52/3ms shot down, 2 crash upon return, and 18 are heavily damaged (unserviceable).
0630	4./KGrzvV 172	6	Two platoons from 6./FJR 2	Paratroop drop near The Hague–Rotterdam highway south of Delft.
0700	KGrzbV 12 (minus 3.Staffel)	38	Rgt Staff IR 65, 6. and 8./IR 65	Infantry assault landing on airfield; 29 Ju 52/3ms shot down or destroyed.
0745	KGrzbV 9 (minus 1.Staffel)	40	22. LL Div Staff, Staff/ Sig Bn 22, Motorcycle Pltn, 13./IR 47, Pltn from 3./Pioneer Bn 22	17 Ju 52/3ms shot down or destroyed. Most others landed off aerodrome, or diverted to other LZs.
1106	IV./KGzbV 1 (minus 16.Staffel); second trip	36	Staff I./IR 65, 1., 2., 3./IR 65	5 Ju 52/3ms shot down or destroyed. 22 diverted to Waalhaven, the rest to Rozenburg Island and Hook of Holland.
1249	KGrzbV 12 (minus 3. Staffel); second trip	38	4./IR 65, 2./FlaK 46	Delayed due to lack of aircraft. Flown by I./KGzbV 172 instead, most landed at Waalhaven.
1429	KGrzbV 9; second trip	40	Staff II./AR 22, 5. and 6./AR 22	Cancelled due to lack of aircraft.
1648	KGrzbV 11; third trip	50	Staff III./AR 22, 7. and 9./AR 22	Cancelled due to lack of aircraft.
1855	KGrzbV 12 (minus 3. Staffel); third trip	40	22. Supply Coy, 1./Med Bn 22	Cancelled due to lack of aircraft.
2102; night flight	KGrzbV 9; third trip	12	5./FlaK 263	Cancelled due to lack of aircraft.
Valkenburg (Landing Zone 1)				
0635	4./KGrzvV 172	6	Two platoons from 6./FJR 2	Paratroop drop on Valkenburg airfield; 2 Ju 52/3m shot down by T.5 bombers (BomVA).
0700	KGrzbV 11	53	Rgt Staff IR 47, 9., 10., 12./IR 47, III Bn Recon Pltn	Infantry assault landing on airfield; 1 Ju 52/3m shot down, 50 destroyed on the airfield, 2 diverted elsewhere.
1105	I./KGzbV 1 (minus 1.Staffel); second trip	39	Staff II./IR 47, 5., 6., 7./IR 47	3 Ju 52/3ms shot down en route to LZ; Valkenburg unusable, 20 return to Werl; 16 land on nearby beaches (1 returns).
1230	KGrzbV 11; second trip	53	Staff/Pi Bn 22, 3./ Pioneer Bn 22(-), Hvy MG Platoon, 2./FlaK 31, Recon Bicycle Sqn	Cancelled due to lack of aircraft.
1636	IV./KGzbV 1; third trip	51	Staff I./IR 47, 1., 2., 3./IR 47, 11./IR 47	Cancelled due to lack of aircraft.
1855	3./KGzbV 12; third trip	12	8./IR 47	Cancelled due to lack of aircraft.
Ockenburg (Landing Zone 3)				
0630	16./KGzbV 1	13	3./FJR 2	Paratroop drop on Ockenburg airfield; 1 Ju 52/3m shot down by AA fire.
0700	3./KGzbV 12	18	Staff II./IR 65, 5./IR 65	Infantry assault landing on airfield; 10 Ju 52/3m shot down or destroyed.
0745	1./KGrzbV 9	15	Bicycle Recon Sqn 2./AR 22	6 Ju 52/3m shot down or destroyed; 4 Ju 52/3m diverted; 1 failed to return/MIA.
1106	16./KGzbV 1; second trip	12	7./IR 65	2 Ju 52/3m diverted to LZ I, both destroyed; 10 Ju 52/3m diverted to Waalhaven.
1249	3./KGzbV 12; second trip	13	Staff/AR 22	Cancelled due to lack of aircraft.
1429	1./KGrzbV 9; second trip	12	13./IR 65	Seven Ju 52/3ms landed at Waalhaven instead; one shot down by Dutch AA fire.
1648	KGrzbV 11; third trip	3	Supply Platoon	Cancelled due to lack of aircraft.

Compiled and translated from German Planning Instructions to 22. LL Infanterie-Division; Attachment to 22. LL Div Operations Officer, Instruction Nr 176/40: 12 April 1940; modified to include known changes to this plan.

Gruppe Süd – the original 'Bridge Too Far'

As Morzik's IV./KGzbV 1 headed for the airfields around The Hague, his other three *Gruppen* fanned out to deliver the aerial assaults intended to secure the three pairs of bridges that would permit the panzers to enter *Vesting Holland* through the 'back door'. Most critical were the long – 1,200m (4,600ft) and 1,400m (4,900ft) respectively – road and railroad bridges spanning the Hollandsch Diep at Moerdijk.

The south ends of these bridges were only lightly guarded – an infantry company (3-III-28e RI) with a dozen MGs and two old 5.7cm guns – since the Dutch planned to withdraw to the north side of the wide estuary and destroy the bridges. But the northern end was defended by four concrete casemates – two of them with 4.7cm A/T guns as well as MGs – manned by a reinforced company of infantry (1-I-28e RI) covered by two artillery battalions (III-14e RA and I-17e RA). AA defence consisted of two Vickers 7.5cm guns and three Spandau MG platoons.

At 0540hrs the Dutch infantry barracks, defensive positions, and AA batteries were pounded by Stukas (IV.(St)/LG 1) for 20 minutes and half an hour later 50 Ju 52/3ms (I./KGzbV 1) rumbled overhead. Two *Fallschirmjäger* companies (II./FJR 1) landed on each side of the kilometre (0.6 mile)-wide waterway and quickly seized both ends of the bridges, removing the demolition charges before they could be used. The Dutch reacted strongly, but in a six-hour pitched battle, the paratroopers overcame the defenders for a loss of two dozen killed and 80 wounded. The lightly armed 6e Grens-Bataljon (Frontier Battalion) counter-attacked from Breda that afternoon but were held off by the paratroopers' machine guns.

As II./FJR 2's 700 *Fallschirmjäger* descended upon the Moerdijk bridges, a dozen Junkers (3./KGrzbV 172) dropped one company of paratroopers (3./FJR 1) at Dordrecht, and one platoon quickly seized the west ends of the highway and railway bridges over the Oude Maas. However, Dordrecht was the home of the 1e Depotcompagnie Pontoniers en Torpedisten (1st Depot Company of Maritime Engineers); the instructors and recruits quickly rallied and in an active defence repulsed the rest of the company, killing 18 and capturing 82.

Dropped by 30 more Junkers (1. and 2./KGrzbV 172), 1. and 2./FJR 1 – along with Oberst Bruno Bräuer, commander of FJR 1, and his 52-man staff – landed between Dordrecht and Moerdijk, neutralizing the Dutch artillery battalions. Immediately Bräuer sent the two companies to Dordrecht where they drove back the Dutch, successfully linking with the 43 men still holding the bridges.

Meanwhile, at Rotterdam the airborne assault on Waalhaven airfield went well in spite of Dutch resistance. The defenders included an infantry and the MG companies from III-Regiment Jäger (III-RJ, 'Jäger' being the legacy title for 'riflemen') manning perimeter defences with the battalion's other two infantry companies positioned on the road into Rotterdam and on the north (harbour) side of the airfield. The base was also defended by three Skoda 75mm heavy AA guns, two Scotti 20mm cannon and a dozen Spandaus.

Two companies of II./FJR 1 landed at either end of the vital Moerdijk railroad and highway bridges spanning the kilometre-wide Holland Deep. In this re-enactment performed for the benefit of Nazi propaganda film crews, the Moerdijk railway bridge is visible in the background to the left. (IWM HU31441)

At 0630hrs 53 Ju 52/3ms (II./KGzbV 1) began delivering 665 paratroopers (III./FJR 1) who quickly secured the airfield, followed only 20 minutes later by 53 more Junkers (III./KGzbV 1) bringing in 630 infantrymen (III./IR 16 staff, 9./IR 16, and three platoons from 2./Pionier-Bataillon 22 [2./Pion.-Bat. 22]). Four of the transports were shot down by G.1 fighters (3e JaVA) and another three were lost to the Dutch AA guns, but the other 46 Junkers managed to land, unload and take off again, as planned, returning to Loddenheide for reinforcements (II./FJR 2).

Immediately following the bombing and strafing attacks on Dutch airfields, some 197 Ju 52/3m tri-motor transports arrived over two strategic bridges, Rotterdam, and the three airfields around The Hague, delivering paratroopers from the 7. Fliegerdivision. The Fokker G.1 above this 'Tante Ju' was added by the Nazi propaganda photo editors. (IWM HU31442)

In an audacious assault, a dozen Heinkel He 59C-2 floatplanes landed 120 infantrymen and pioneers from 22. Luftlande-Division on the Nieuwe Maas River in downtown Rotterdam. The troops captured the road and railway bridges spanning the river and held them until Student's main forces could arrive. (NIMH)

Within an hour and a half, the paratroopers had eliminated three of the Jäger companies and all the AA guns, allowing the infantrymen to organize and move out for the two bridges spanning the Nieuwe Maas. The Jäger battalion commander – who had already lost 58 killed and 600 captured – ordered a retreat, but his remaining troops (3-III-RJ) were so panicked that only 100 men regrouped and these withdrew to join the Rotterdam garrison forces.

Meanwhile, the bridges had been seized by 90 men of the reinforced 11./IR 16 (bolstered with two MG squads and a platoon from 2./Pion.-Bat. 22) audaciously flown into the heart of Rotterdam by 12 elderly He 59C-2 twin-engine float biplanes. Landing on the water's surface at 0610hrs, they taxied up to Noordereiland ('Northern Island'), in the middle of the river, where the troops clambered ashore to capture the large Willemsbrug ('William [of Orange] Bridge') and the smaller Spoorbrug railroad bridge connecting the island to the two halves of the city. They overwhelmed the surprised guards, disconnected the demolition charges and began setting up defensive positions. Three dozen paratroopers (11./FJR 1) dropped into south Rotterdam's Feyenoord sports stadium quickly arrived in a convoy of commandeered automobiles led by a confiscated streetcar. Shortly afterwards local Dutch forces – two companies from III-39e RI – deployed and raked the bridgehead with intense small-arms and machine-gun fire, isolating half of the 126-man detachment and preventing any further reinforcement.

Several spirited counter-attacks – most notably by three sections of Dutch marines – failed to dislodge the invaders, so Winkelman's HQ ordered the navy to bombard the Germans holding the Willemsbrug. Vice-Admiraal Johannes Furstner dispatched the old World War I torpedo boat *Z-5* and new Vosper MTB *TM-51* from Hoek van Holland and sent the 1,650-ton destroyer *Van Galen* from

Den Helder. Entering the battle at 0800hrs, the *Z-5* engaged German positions at point-blank range (100m) with its 75mm Bofors and flamed four of Staffel Schwilden's He 59C-2 floatplanes before withdrawing, its ammunition exhausted and having suffered five casualties from German MG fire and hits by the sole Rheinmetall 3.7cm PaK36 A/T gun delivered in the first wave. *Van Galen* arrived mid-afternoon and soon became the primary target for 12 Ju 87s (IV.(St)/LG 2). Trapped in the narrow confines of the Nieuwe Waterweg and unable to manoeuvre,

The Dutch destroyer *Van Galen*. (NIMH)

she was severely damaged, her hull being ruptured by near misses. Run aground in Merwede harbour and abandoned in a sinking condition, she was finished off by KG 4's He 111s.

Meanwhile the landing of Junkers transports at Waalhaven continued unabated, 22 Ju 52/3ms (IV./KGzbV 1) arriving at 1125hrs. Unable to land at Ypenburg, these offloaded 330 Luftlande troops (two companies I./IR 65). Five minutes later, III./KGzbV 1 returned with Student, his 60-man staff, and two companies of paratroopers (5. and 7./FJR 2), followed shortly afterwards by II./KGzbV 1, 32 Junkers delivering four Skoda 7.5cm GebK15 mountain howitzers (7. Fallschirmschützbatterie), three A/T platoons (7. Pakkompanie), and six FlaK 38 2cm AA guns (lichte Flakbatterie 106). The huge numbers of transports clogging Waalhaven presented a perfect target and a battalion of 10.5cm howitzers (I-10e RA) took them under fire, the 675 shell bombardment destroying 11 aircraft, with another five shot down by ground fire.

To further disrupt the Luftwaffe's arrivals, Winkelman directed the ML – and requested the RAF – to bomb the airfield. To avoid civilian casualties, the RAF instead sent six Blenheim IF 'heavy fighters' (600 Sqn), but these were intercepted by their Luftwaffe equivalent (Bf 110Cs of 3./ZG 1) and five were shot down. The ML followed at 1325hrs with five C.10s (StratVerVA) attacking with 40 110 lb (50kg) bombs – destroying another Ju 52/3m – then losing two to Bf 109Es (7./JG 3) intercepting them on egress. Two hours later three (of four remaining) T.5 bombers, escorted by six D.21s (2e JaVA), also struck, destroying three just-landed Ju 52/3ms (Stab/KGzbV 2) amongst the 40 transports (I./KGrzbV 172) off-loading 332 infantrymen and a FlaK battery (4./IR 65 and Flak-Bttr 2./46). Also intercepted during egress, the Dutch lost two bombers and two escorts to the marauding Messerschmitts (6./JG 27).

The RAF's final daylight attack struck at 1620hrs when nine Blenheim IV's (15 Sqn) eluded interception and attacked while six KGrzvV 9 transports were offloading 63 men and four 7.5cm leIG18 infantry guns (14./IR 65), destroying one Junkers and two guns. During the night the RAF hit the embattled airfield with four waves of nine Vickers Wellington medium bombers (No. 3 Group) that knocked out Waalhaven altogether – destroying a further 13 Ju 52/3ms.

But by the end of the day Gruppe Süd had massed 3,700 troops at Rotterdam and Student began dispatching elements of his command to hold the vital bridges against the Dutch counter-attacks sure to come. It would be at least three more days before Küchler's panzers arrived and only then if they were not delayed by Giraud's approaching 7e Armée.

Additionally, Student's airlift units had suffered severe losses. The two transport wings had lost 149 Ju 52/3ms destroyed and another 83 damaged and abandoned where they landed, plus another 34 damaged and declared unserviceable upon return to base. (In the five-day campaign, KGzbV 1 lost 63 of its 208 Ju 52/3ms and KGzbV 2 lost 157 of 204. Of the 83 aircraft abandoned in Holland, 53 were later recovered and repaired to airworthy condition.) This left only 194 Ju 52/3ms available for resupply and reinforcements airlifts.

While Sponeck's attempted *coup de main* had been an unmitigated failure, Student's operation was a qualified success. His 7. Fliegerdivision and IR 16 had captured all three pairs of bridges, but the 60 paratroopers and Luftlande infantry holding the north ends of the Rotterdam bridges were cut off, Dutch defences were rapidly being reinforced, and crossing the bridges was – for the time being – suicidal. The Germans had not 'kicked in the door', but they did have a foot stuck in it.

Meanwhile, at the frontier

Gruppe Süd's successful air assaults at Rotterdam suddenly made that city the key to *Vesting Holland*'s defence, so Winkleman reinforced Kolonel Pieter W. Scharroo's small garrison with a regiment from the Veldleger's 4e Divisie and a battalion from his reserve. (These were 11e RI, with its HQ, one battalion, and its A/T and mortar companies, with two battalions from 2e Division's 10e and 15e RIs, and III-21e RI from Leiden.) That afternoon Winkelman also withdrew most of 2e Esk Paw's armoured cars from the Grebbe Line, sending one platoon to augment 4e RI attacking Luftlande troops at Valkenburg, another to assist the grenadiers at Overschie, and the third to support the marines' renewed attacks on the Germans' Rotterdam bridgehead.

Tasked with recapturing Waalhaven airfield in an attack planned to follow the RAF's night bombardment, the Light Division's 2e Regiment Wielrijders (2e RW) arrived at Alblasserdam just before midnight on 10/11 May, but Kolonel Hendrik van der Bijl decided to wait until daylight before crossing the Noord waterway. By that time, Student had dispatched two infantry companies (5. and 6./IR 16) and a pair of leIG18 infantry guns to hold the Alblasserdam bridge and, the next day, the bicyclist infantry's piecemeal crossing attempts were repeatedly repulsed.

Because Waalhaven was unusable due to the RAF bombings, Student's reinforcements had to be landed on the Rotterdam–Dordrecht motorway. On their first mission 35 Ju 52/3ms (KGrzbV 9) delivered two companies of infantry (9./IR 65 and 1./IR 72) and their battalion staffs, the transports returning late in the afternoon with additional infantry

Waalhaven the morning after, Ju 52/3ms destroyed and damaged by RAF and ML air attacks littering the airfield. (Bundesarchiv Bild 141-1308)

(IR 47) and some light artillery (AR 22). Using 100 confiscated Dutch trucks, Student sent III./FJR 1, 7./IR 16, three Skoda 7.5cm GebK15 mountain howitzers, and a platoon of 3.7cm PaK 36 A/T guns to Dordrecht.

Responding to the isolated Luftlande units' need for air support, Kesselring assigned Putzier three *Stukagruppen* (StG 77) while KG 4 Heinkels flew repeated missions bombing Dutch artillery batteries and troop columns. Assuring air superiority, JG 51 patrolled Dutch skies, while JG 26 covered northern Belgium.

Meanwhile, in the east, the Dutch expected five infantry battalions (35e and 43e RI), fighting from riverside casemates, MG pillboxes, and the ancient Fort Westervoort, to delay the invaders for 24 hours at the IJssel River. Spearheading the thrust towards Arnhem, the Austrian SS motorized regiment Der Führer (SS-DF, detached from SS-Verfügungs Division), backed by 207. Infanterie-Division's troops and artillery, was repulsed twice before finally forcing a crossing at Doesburg eight hours later. Arnhem fell that afternoon and, further delayed by repeated encounters with the horse-mounted 4e Halfregiment Huzaren, the motorized SS troops finally entered Wageningen by nightfall. Meanwhile SS Leibstandarte Adolf Hitler ('Bodyguards of Adolf Hitler', abbreviated SS-LAH), led 227. Infanterie-Division to the IJssel and, following repulses elsewhere, forced their way across the river at Zutphen late in the day.

Early the next morning, SS-DF assaulted the forward positions of the Grebbe Line, but made little progress. The following day (12 May), after a nine-hour artillery bombardment – Dutch artillery was singularly ineffective in counter-battery fire – the stormtroopers repeatedly attacked the Dutch defences (8e RI), slowly but steadily moving up the Grebbeberg against stubborn resistance.

A Dutch counter-attack at 0840hrs the next morning (13 May) by two battalions from Brigade Group B (I- and III-29e RI) began promisingly, supported by two small ML raids that bombed and strafed German artillery positions and vehicle parks near Wageningen. However, it quickly collapsed in the face of murderous MG fire from SS-DF, heavy artillery barrages, and a horrendous pounding by 27 Stukas (StG 77). Meanwhile, a regiment of 207. Infanterie-Division (IR 207) resumed the Grebbeberg assaults, and in a four-hour battle finally destroyed the defending unit (8e RI, which lost 425 KIA), capturing the summit. With the Grebbe Line crumbling, Luitenant-Generaal Jan Joseph Baron van Voorst tot Voorst ordered a withdrawal to the secondary defensive line, the 'Nieuwe Hollandse Waterlinie' (NHW) centred on Utrecht.

In the north-east, the 1. Kavallerie-Division made little progress against Dutch frontier battalions on the first day, but afterwards three cavalry regiments quickly rode across the three north-eastern provinces, arriving at Stavoren and the Wons Line, the outer defence of the Afsluitdijk's eastern end. The defenders consisted of five infantry companies (I-33e RI reinforced) fighting from earthworks and pillboxes with KM gunboats providing naval gunfire support.

Despite its advanced mechanization, the German Army retained one division of traditional horse-mounted cavalry. This extraneous, obsolete unit found its purpose in advancing across Drenthe, Groningen, and Friesland to attack Fort Kornwerderzand, guarding the eastern terminus of the Afsluitdijk causeway. (IWM RML225)

German soldiers crossing the Maas River. (NIMH)

Preceded by artillery barrages (RAB 1) and Luftwaffe strafing (6.[J]/TrGr 186), the dismounted cavalry (RR 1 and 2) began attacking at 1340hrs. After three hours of bombardment, strafing, and assaults, the defence crumbled, but the attackers were stopped by the casemated guns of Fort Kornwerderzand. During and afterwards Stukas sank two gunboats and damaged a third.

In the south-east, each of the eight bridges spanning the Maas from Roermond to Grave was guarded by an infantry company fighting from a couple of concrete casemates and 10–12 MG pillboxes. Mostly local reservists, each company was also equipped with a Böhler 4.7cm A/T gun, an ancient Krupp 8.4cm 'infantry gun' and a mortar section. Alerted by frontier troops as the Germans crossed the border, the fortifications were manned by the time the invaders reached the river and – with one disastrous exception – the bridges were all 'blown' and the defenders fought tenaciously, repulsing repeated river crossing attempts until the attackers began using Luftwaffe 8.8cm FlaK 36/37s firing directly into the gun embrasures. By midday several successful crossings had been made and, by 1600hrs, the Maas Line crumbled.

The exception was at Gennep where a team of commandos, impersonating Dutch military police escorting a group of 'captured Germans', surprised and overwhelmed the guards, seizing the railway bridge and removing the demolition charges. Minutes later a *Panzerzug* (armoured train) crossed the bridge, followed by a 23-car freight train carrying a 750-man infantry battalion (III./IR 481) that steamed through the Peel Line and halted at Mill, two miles (3km) to the west.

With the invaders behind them, the defenders – one infantry battalion (I-3e RI) manning 47 MG pillboxes and supported by an artillery battalion (III-20e RA) – were at a severe tactical disadvantage. The 2e RHM was sent from the Lichte Divisie to repulse the penetration, but the 350-man motorcycle unit proved inadequate, especially when the rest of IR 481 arrived at midday, followed by another regiment (IR 456) six hours later. By midnight, two Dutch infantry battalions had been destroyed, 2e RHM had suffered heavy casualties, and a mile-wide (1.6km) gap had been blown in the Peel Line. Two hours later the commander of the ad hoc 'Peel Division', Kolonel Leonard Schmidt, ordered his battalions to retreat behind the Zuid-Willemsvaart Canal. (The 'Peel Division' was a collection of two infantry regiments, two frontier battalions, and battalions taken from each of the six infantry regiments making up IIIe Legerkorps, supported by a regiment of 36 obsolete 8.4cm field guns. Its mission was to delay the Germans long enough for IIIe Legerkorps to withdraw into *Vesting Holland*.)

The morning's dramatic penetration of the Peel Line prompted Winkelman to order the immediate withdrawal of IIIe Legerkorps, the Lichte Divisie travelling to Alblasserdam and the other two divisions manning the riverside defences from Ochten to Gorinchem. Nearly simultaneously, the news that

AOK 18's invasion of the Netherlands, 10–13 May 1940.

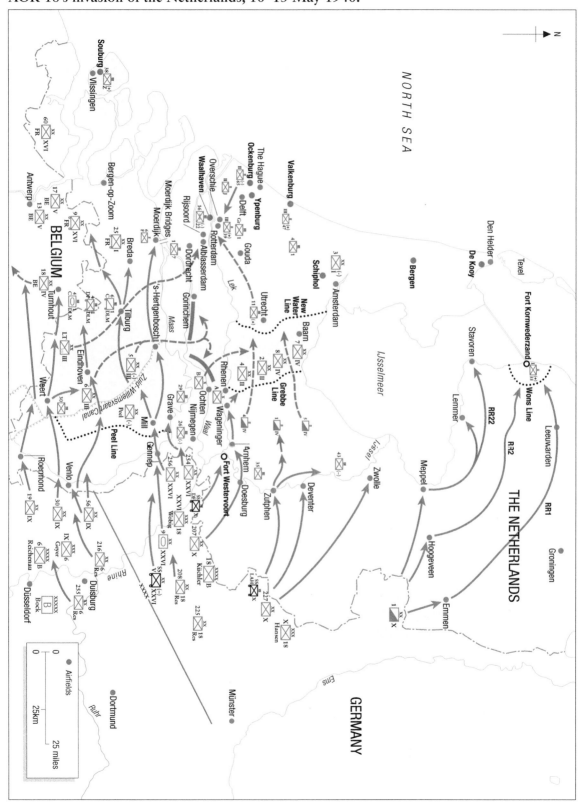

the *Panzerzug* had penetrated to Mill caused XXVI AK commander Generalleutnant Albert Wobig to order the 9. Panzer-Division into action, followed closely by SS-Verfügungs Division's motorized infantry.

As Hubicki's panzers drove through Gennep and Mill that night, Schmidt was encouraged by meeting Colonel Pierre Dario, commanding the French 6e Cuirassiers, the armoured car regiment of Général François Picard's 1ère DLM, which had just arrived at Tilburg. The two colonels – allies at last – agreed to form a collective defence where the 'Peel Division's' remaining battalions held the lines Hertogenbosch to Tilburg and Dario's regiment deployed from Tilburg to Turnhout, Belgium. But, changing orders caused confusion and as Schmidt's lightly armed foot soldiers straggled northwards, they were quickly overrun and scattered by Hubicki's hard-charging panzers. Chaos reigned as panicked troops fled westwards, the panzers entered Tilburg, and Schmidt and his staff were captured that morning. With 223 men killed and 18,000 captured in three days, the 'Peel Division' was destroyed.

The French 7e Armée had indeed arrived overnight. The 25e Division d'Infanterie Motorisée (25e DIM) deployed from Breda southwards, Lieutenant Colonel Denis, commanding 38e Régiment d'Infanterie Motorisée, ordering the city's 40,000 residents to evacuate into Belgium. Driving directly to Moerdijk were a platoon of Dario's Panhard 178 armoured cars, two platoons of motorcyclists, and a squadron of motorized infantry (200 troops from 12e GRDI), soon joined by two more platoons of Panhards (5e GRDIm) escorting Général Eugene Desité Antoinne Mittelhauser, Gamelin's liaison officer to the Dutch High Command. Meeting the Dutch 6e Grens-Bataljon at Zevenbergen, the 15 Panhards scouted the paratroopers' positions at the south end of the bridges, attracting the Luftwaffe's attention. A Heinkel raid (III./KG 4) devastated the village, killing five French soldiers and 32 civilians, and (correctly) believing they lacked the combat power to retake the bridges, the French retired to the west.

Panzers to the rescue

With the 'Peel Division' destroyed and the French driven from Moerdijk, the way was opened for Hubicki's 9. Panzer-Division to ride to the paratroopers' rescue. Covered by JG 26's Messerschmitts and learning from Luftwaffe aerial reconnaissance that the French had deployed before him, Hubicki formed three 'pursuit groups'. Gefechtsgruppe Lüttwitz – Oberstleutnant Heinrich Freiherr von Lüttwitz's Aufklärungs-Regiment (mot.) 9 and a company of motorized riflemen – drove to Moerdijk ahead of Gefechtsgruppe Apell (I./Panzer Regiment 33 [PzR 33] and Schützen Regiment 10, led by Oberst Wilhelm von

Apell, 9. Schützen-Brigade commander). Meanwhile the Gefechtsgruppe Sponeck (II./PzR 33 and Schützen Regiment 11, under SR 11 commander, Oberst Theodor von Sponeck) advanced towards Tilburg and Breda. While Sponeck drove the French Panhards from Tilburg, Gefechtsgruppe Lüttwitz hurried west, its SdKfz 221/232 armoured cars crossing the Moerdijk bridge at 1825hrs, linking with the paratroopers. Thirty minutes later they joined Bräuer's FJR 1, which was having a difficult time battling the Lichte Divisie.

In an ambitious attempt to reach Waalhaven via Dordrecht, van der Bijl sent four battalions of bicycle infantry (2e RW plus II-1e RW) and eight Krupp 7.5cm field guns (II-KRA) across the Merwede waterway to launch a major attack at midday on 12 May. The western wing soon stalled in vicious street fighting against III./FJR 1 and the eastern wing was halted by a flanking counter-attack by recently arrived reinforcements (I./IR 72) while supporting artillery (25e BA) was bombed by KG 4. The arrival of Lüttwitz's armoured cars caused several Dutch units to panic and flee, and the rest of the exhausted bicycle infantry withdrew behind a canal in Dordrecht's old city centre.

Learning that the major portion of Hubicki's 9. Panzer-Division was 12–18 hours behind Lüttwitz's detachment, at 0240hrs the next morning, Winkelman ordered artillery and aerial bombardments to destroy the Moerdijk bridges. The local artillery – 25e BA's seven surviving Krupp 15cm 'fortress guns' – proved inadequate and the ML's last remaining T.5 bomber missed the bridges with both 661 lb (300kg) bombs, and then it and an escorting G.1 were shot down by Bf 109Es (4./JG 26); all aboard were killed.

That morning (13 May) Gefechtsgruppe Apell crossed the Moerdijk bridge and entered Dordrecht, one company of panzers driving directly into the barricaded/fortified portion of the city. Immediately vicious urban combat erupted. Dutch Böhler 4.7cm A/T guns and Krupp 7.5cm field pieces – firing over open sights down short, narrow streets – destroyed two PzKpfw IIs and one PzKpfw III and disabled three other tanks, but the defenders were driven away from the bridges and the riflemen's 'thin-skinned' personnel carriers drove on to Rotterdam unimpeded.

Sponeck's *Gefechtsgruppe* arrived at Breda and engaged Dario's Panhards, supporting SS-Verfügungs Division's attacks against the French 38e Régiment d'Infanterie (38e RI). As General der Infanterie Hermann Geyer's IX AK approached Turnhout, the Belgian 18eme Division withdrew across the Albert Canal, exposing the 1ére DLM's right flank, so Picard retreated as well.

Following Hubicki's panzers to Rijsoord (Student's HQ between Dordrecht and Rotterdam) was Generalleutnant Rudolf Schmidt and his XXXIX AK staff. At midday Küchler reorganized his army, assigning to Schmidt all of Student's forces, 9. Panzer-Division, 254. Infanterie-Division, and SS-LAH. Wobig's XXVI AK, now consisting of 256. Infanterie-Division and SS-Verfügungs Division, was reinforced with two companies of Hubicki's panzers and 208. and 225. Infanterie-Divisionen. Vastly outnumbered and with little air cover, Général Molinié's 25e DIM withdrew to Bergen op Zoom to defend the Scheldt Estuary.

In an ambitious attempt to drive to Waalhaven by breaking the *Fallschirmjägers'* hold on Dordrecht, the Lichte Divisie's lightly armed bicycle infantry deployed four battalions and initially made strong advances against the equally lightly equipped paratroopers. (NIMH)

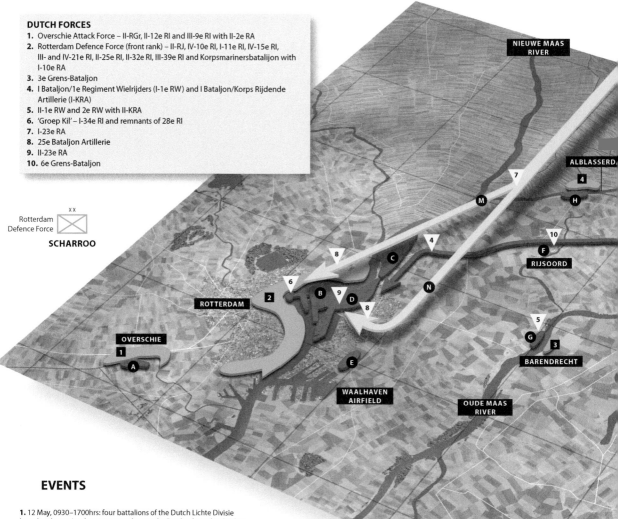

DUTCH FORCES

1. Overschie Attack Force – II-RGr, II-12e RI and III-9e RI with II-2e RA
2. Rotterdam Defence Force (front rank) – II-RJ, IV-10e RI, I-11e RI, IV-15e RI, III- and IV-21e RI, II-25e RI, II-32e RI, III-39e RI and Korpsmarinersbataljon with I-10e RA
3. 3e Grens-Bataljon
4. I Bataljon/1e Regiment Wielrijders (I-1e RW) and I Bataljon/Korps Rijdende Artillerie (I-KRA)
5. II-1e RW and 2e RW with II-KRA
6. 'Groep Kil' – I-34e RI and remnants of 28e RI
7. I-23e RA
8. 25e Bataljon Artillerie
9. II-23e RA
10. 6e Grens-Bataljon

Rotterdam Defence Force

SCHARROO

NIEUWE MAAS RIVER

ALBLASSERD.

RIJSOORD

ROTTERDAM

OVERSCHIE

BARENDRECHT

WAALHAVEN AIRFIELD

OUDE MAAS RIVER

EVENTS

1. 12 May, 0930–1700hrs: four battalions of the Dutch Lichte Divisie launch a determined counter-attack to retake Dordrecht and its bridges. 'Groep Kil' is poised to cross the Dordtsche Kil as soon as the bicycle battalions reach Zeehaven. However, Dutch attacks stall following a flanking counter-attack by I./IR 72, beginning at 1400hrs.

2. 1745hrs: Gefechtsgruppe Lüttwitz (Aufkl-Rgt 9[+]) arrives at Moerdijk perimeter. Crossing the bridge at 1825hrs, Lüttwitz reports to Oberst Bräuer's CP in Dordrecht 30 minutes later.

3. 13 May, midday: Gefechtsgruppe Apell (I./PzR 33 and SR 10) arrives at Dordrecht. At 1600hrs one panzer company (20 tanks of all four marks) engages Dutch defenders in the city centre while the remaining panzers and SR 10 cross the bridge to Zwijndrecht, headed for Rotterdam. At 2040hrs the Lichte Divisie withdraws to Alblasserdam.

4. 1400–2000hrs: I./PzR 33 and SR 10 arrive in south Rotterdam. XXXIX AK (mot.) takes command of Student's forces in the Rotterdam area. Planning begins for the cross-river assault to be launched the next day.

5. 2040hrs: one panzer platoon (one PzKpfw III and three PzKpfw IIs) reinforces the infantry at Barendrecht bridge and despite losses forces 3e Grens-Bataljon to retreat.

6. 14 May, 1120hrs: with forces reorganized (Kampfgruppen A, B, and C) and deployed for a cross-river assault scheduled for 1530hrs, Schmidt begins negotiations with Scharroo for surrender of the city. Due to promising progress, at 1415hrs Schmidt signals Luftflotte 2 to cancel the pre-assault bombardment.

7. 1430hrs: unaware of Kesselring's 'abort attack' order, KG 54 approaches from the east and splits into two attack groups. Initially, red flares fired from the bridges – signalling abort the attack – are not seen.

8. 1440hrs: KG 54's main group attacks as planned. I./KG 54 sees the red flares and aborts its attack; only three aircraft release bombs.

9. 1730hrs: Scharroo surrenders the city, PzR 33 and SS-LAH cross the bridges into Rotterdam. Shortly afterwards Student is wounded by 'friendly fire' from an SS motorcycle battalion.

10. 15 May, 1145hrs: at Schmidt's HQ in Rijsoord, Winkelman and Küchler sign the armistice, Winkelman surrendering all Dutch forces under his command.

PANZERS TO THE RESCUE, 12–14 MAY 1940

On 12 May 1940 the Dutch 'Light Division' attempted to dislodge the German paratroopers' hold on the Dordrecht bridges, but was defeated by a timely flanking counter-attack. The following morning leading elements of the 9. Panzer Division arrived, eliminating the threat at Dordrecht, and made contact with Student's forces at Rotterdam. A Luftwaffe air attack on 14 May ended all resistance; Rotterdam surrendered, and shortly after the Dutch capitulated.

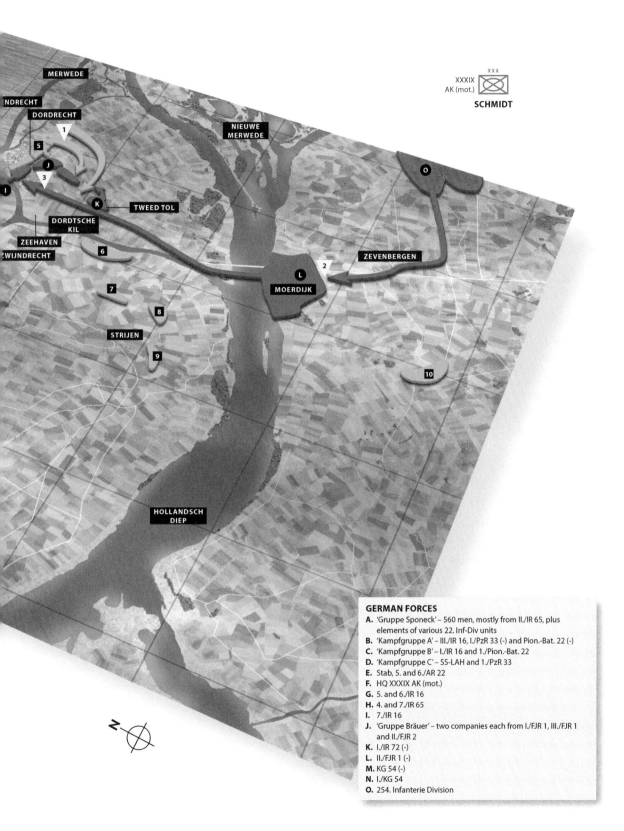

XXXIX
AK (mot.)

XXX

SCHMIDT

MERWEDE

NDRECHT

DORDRECHT

NIEUWE
MERWEDE

1

5

J

3

I

K

TWEED TOL

DORDTSCHE
KIL

ZEEHAVEN

ZWIJNDRECHT

6

7

8

STRIJEN

9

O

2

ZEVENBERGEN

L

MOERDIJK

10

HOLLANDSCH
DIEP

N

GERMAN FORCES
A. 'Gruppe Sponeck' – 560 men, mostly from II./IR 65, plus
elements of various 22. Inf-Div units
B. 'Kampfgruppe A' – III./IR 16, I./PzR 33 (-) and Pion.-Bat. 22 (-)
C. 'Kampfgruppe B' – I./IR 16 and 1./Pion.-Bat. 22
D. 'Kampfgruppe C' – SS-LAH and 1./PzR 33
E. Stab, 5. and 6./AR 22
F. HQ XXXIX AK (mot.)
G. 5. and 6./IR 16
H. 4. and 7./IR 65
I. 7./IR 16
J. 'Gruppe Bräuer' – two companies each from I./FJR 1, III./FJR 1
and II./FJR 2
K. I./IR 72 (-)
L. II./FJR 1 (-)
M. KG 54 (-)
N. I./KG 54
O. 254. Infanterie Division

With Küchler's army having fully invested 'Fortress Holland' and the Veldleger regrouping on the NWL, the Dutch government knew it was time to evacuate if the war was to be continued from foreign soil. In its most meaningful contribution, the MLD used a T.8W twin-engine reconnaissance floatplane to fly two cabinet members – Foreign Minister Eelco van Kleffens and Colonial Minister Charles Welter – to the UK on the first day of the invasion. Three days later three British destroyers spirited away the Queen, royal family, and Cabinet. Additionally, at midday on 14 May, Furstner and the KM were ordered to withdraw to Britain to continue the struggle, ground forces in Zeeland (astride the Scheldt Estuary) being reassigned to Furstner so that they could continue defensive operations in the event Winkelman capitulated.

Meanwhile at Rijsoord, Schmidt prepared a full-force cross-river assault, primarily using III./IR 16, supported by I./PzR 33, with I./IR 16 crossing the Nieuwe Maas in barges upstream to begin an envelopment. By this time Hubicki had lost 17 tanks – nine PzKpfw I/IIs, three PzKpfw IIIs, and five PzKpfw IVs (only two of these in action against French units) – and was concerned about suffering further losses to Dutch A/T guns. Since he and Student had little artillery, strong Stuka support was requested. However, at noon that day Richthofen's Fliegerkorps VIII was reassigned to Luftflotte 3 to assist Guderian at Sedan, Reinhardt at Monthermé, and Rommel at Dinant, so none were available. Kesselring gave the mission to KG 54 and a liaison officer flew into Waalhaven that evening to coordinate the pre-assault bombardment. The preparatory air bombardment would hit at 1440hrs the next day, followed by an artillery barrage at 1500hrs, and the assault would commence at 1530hrs.

Defending Rotterdam Colonel Pieter Wilhelmus Scharroo had about 10,000 men (18 infantry battalions), a dozen 10.5cm howitzers, three A/T guns and a pair of armoured cars. All the AA guns had been withdrawn to defend The Hague and the ML was reduced to nine serviceable D.21s with no early warning capability whatsoever. Most significantly, the Dutch – not yet acquainted with the totality and horror of modern war – failed to evacuate the city.

Winkelman, meanwhile, attempted to secure the national redoubt, launching a three-battalion (II-RGr, III-9e RI, and II-12e RI) attack on the 560 airborne troops – now including General Sponeck's group from Ockenburg – hunkered down in Overschie. Additionally, Winkelman organized blocking forces at Delft and Gouda to prevent a breakout from Rotterdam from reaching The Hague or attacking the rear of the Veldleger on the NHW.

Hoping to preclude the need for a costly cross-river assault and bloody urban combat, at 1040hrs Schmidt

After brushing aside two French infantry battalions and two reconnaissance groups, the 9. Panzer-Division finally crossed the Holland Deep and headed for Rotterdam to relieve Student's exhausted air assault troops holding the south side of the city. (Ryan Noppen)

sent a surrender ultimatum to Scharroo, who received it 40 minutes later. After conferring with Winkelman, who needed time to complete the operation at Overschie and his preparations at Delft and Gouda, Scharroo rejected the ultimatum on technical grounds. Schmidt quickly prepared a technically correct replacement and, sensing it would be accepted, contacted Kesselring at 1415hrs to cancel the air attack. However, KG 54's 90 He 111Ps had taken off at 1345hrs and, with communications of the day being cumbersome and slow, the abort order was not received by Lackner before the bombers' retracted their HF radio aerials approaching the target area.

The Wehrmacht's campaign in Holland ended as it began, with a devastating bombing attack by Heinkel He 111s. (NIMH)

Approaching from the east at 2,300ft (700m), Lackner split his *Geschwader* into two formations, leading the larger one (II. and III./KG 54) directly ahead while 36 others (I./KG 54) angled left to attack from the south. The criss-crossing bomb paths were designed to avoid hitting the 50 troops holding the bridgehead while isolating the Dutch frontline defenders from reinforcements, thus limiting the opposition to Schmidt's assault. Realizing the bombers were inbound, Student had red flares fired to warn them off. Lackner's formation did not see them, but most of the second wave aborted. In all 57 Heinkels dropped 67.7 tons of bombs, gutting the medieval city centre and killing 814 civilians. At 1730hrs, Scharroo surrendered.

Accompanied by Student, I./PzR 33 and III./IR 16 immediately hurried across the Willemsbrug to secure the city, with SS-LAH's motorcycle battalion following. Encountering a group of Dutch troops being disarmed, the stormtroopers opened fire, the fusillade wounding Student in the head. His life was saved by a Dutch surgeon.

While the devastating air raid was ordered, planned, and executed as a tactical strike, Nazi leadership immediately elevated it to an act of terror. Propaganda leaflets scattered across Utrecht announced that if that city did not surrender, it would also 'suffer the fate of Warsaw'. Knowing that the Luftwaffe's bombers could not be stopped, at 1830hrs Winkelman surrendered to prevent other Dutch cities from suffering Rotterdam's fate.

Late the next morning Winkelman met Küchler at his Rijsoord HQ to sign the armistice. Wisely, he surrendered only the forces under his command, not the nation itself. Meanwhile, in London, Queen Wilhelmina established the Dutch government in exile and vowed to continue the fight until able to return to the Netherlands.

With the pall of the burning city hanging in the air and severely restricting visibility, Hubicki's panzers drove across the Willemsbrug and into Rotterdam, finally relieving Sponeck's beleaguered air assault forces. (NIMH)

THE 'MATADOR'S CLOAK'

When the news came that the enemy was advancing along the whole front I could have wept for joy: they'd fallen into the trap!

Adolf Hitler, 18 October 1940

The Luftwaffe strikes Belgium: 10 May

At 0425hrs on 10 May, an hour before the first wave of Luftwaffe transports crossed the Dutch border headed for bridges and airfields in Holland, another 41 Ju 52/3ms (17./KGzbV 5) began taking off from two airfields near Köln. (For security purposes this four-staffel transport group was assigned a squadron designation – 17th Staffel of the 5th Transport Geschwader – thus making it seem a much smaller unit than it actually was.) Lifting off in sections of three – and each trimotor dragging a heavily laden DFS 230 assault glider into the air – with 30 seconds between sections, the entire formation was airborne within five minutes. They circled once over Köln, clawing for altitude, before heading south-west following a dotted line of bonfire beacons and vertically pointing searchlights. An unexpected tailwind scooted the train of transports along so that, as they climbed to their 8,530ft (2,600m) release altitude, they crossed into Dutch airspace before signalling the glider pilots to release their tow-lines.

Upon release, the 37 DFS gliders (four had become separated from their tow-planes en route) fanned out in four streams towards their targets: three bridges spanning the Albert Canal west of Maastricht and Fort Eben Emael. While the glider assault that neutralized the fort was dramatic and sensational – and demoralizing to the Allies – it was only the enabling adjunct to accomplishing 'Sturmabteilung Koch's' primary mission – seizing the bridges (see Osprey Fortress 30: *Fort Eben Emael* and Osprey Raid 38: *The Fall of Eben Emael*). With the three bridges secured, the gateways into central Belgium would be opened for Hoepner's panzers to race towards Gembloux.

The northern two bridges – Vroenhoven and Veldwezelt – were defended by detachments of Escadron des Cyclistes-Frontière, commanded by Capitaine-commandant Giedelo, whose command post (CP) was in the unit's casern in nearby Lanaken. Crossing above the descending gliders, at 0520hrs four Ju 87Bs arrived over the small town and located the casern. Winging over into screaming dives they demolished Giedelo's CP, killing him and 20 others, just as he was preparing orders to 'blow the bridges'.

The steel bridge at Vroenhoven – carrying the Maastricht–Tongeren/Namur road across the canal – was the most important and it was attacked by ten gliders delivering Hauptmann Walter Koch, his 25-man staff and 96 assault troops, the first glider landing at 0519hrs. Landing close

Hitler, with the officers of Sturmabteilung Koch after presenting each with the Ritterkreuz. Koch is standing to Hitler's immediate right. (André Wilderdijk)

behind the defenders, the attackers had no trouble overwhelming them, Koch signalling 'mission accomplished' 11 minutes later. To the north, starting at 0524hrs nine gliders landed 92 men – ten of them injured in a hard landing – near the Veldwezelt bridge. They, too, quickly overwhelmed the defenders, killing a dozen in the bunker defending the west end of the bridge and reporting 'objective taken' nine minutes after landing. Having lost 15 killed, the two detachments dug in and at 0615hrs they and the detachment at Kanne were reinforced by

The Belgians weren't the only ones using biplanes. The Luftwaffe's three-squadron Schlachtgruppe (II.[Schl]/LG 2) employed 38 Henschel Hs 123 attack aircraft, their superior manoeuvrability proving advantageous in breaking up Belgian infantry counter-attacks at the Albert Canal bridges. (Thijs Postma)

33 more paratroopers – three machine-gun squads – dropped by six Ju 52/3ms and supplied with ammunition by three He 111s. Repulsing a series of desperate, sporadic counter-attacks, they killed 257 Belgian troops (2eme Carabinier and 18eme Ligne regiments).

The southern bridge, near Kanne, was attacked by nine gliders bearing 80 troops – one of the gliders being riddled by machine-gun fire during its approach. Early-morning mist scattered the gliders, delaying the ground attack and resulting in loss of surprise. The defenders resisted fiercely and destroyed the bridge before it could be captured. Flying in relays, Richthofen's five *Stukagruppen* (StGs 2 and 77) and one with Hs 123A assault biplanes (II.[Schlact]/LG 2) provided almost continuous close air support, striking Belgian artillery positions (8eme RA) and shattering the 2eme Grenadiers' counter-attack, killing 216 troops. Isolated, Koch's Kanne detachment lost 22 killed, one captured and 26 wounded before being relieved the next morning.

While Richthofen's Stukas directly supported the airborne assaults along the Albert Canal, his Do 17Zs (KG 77) decimated the Belgian AéM's fighter force in fierce low-level airfield attacks. Preparing for gunnery exercises, at the main fighter base, Schaffen-Diest, the 2eme Regiment d'Aéronautique's Gladiators and Hurricanes (Groupe I) were joined by a dozen obsolete Fairey Fox VI/VIII two-seat reconnaissance-fighter biplanes (Escadrille 5/III/2) and nine Fairey Fox VIC light bombers (7/III/3). Alerted at 0300hrs but grounded by early-morning fog until 0530hrs, the Fox fighters were finally able to take off, and the Glosters and Hawkers were preparing to do so, when – two minutes later – the Dornier twin-engine bombers came roaring in at tree-top height. Eight Hurricanes, two Gladiators and seven Fox VICs were destroyed on the ground. Two Hurricanes escaped to Beauvechain, where they – along with the last Hawker at Schaffen – were destroyed in follow-up attacks.

From Nivelles, the two squadrons of Fiat CR.42s (Groupe II) took to the air and flew to Brustem, avoiding a raid by nine Stukas (4./StG 2) at 0630hrs that destroyed three hangared Fiats, two Foxes, and ten Fairey Firefly trainers. However, that afternoon more Ju 87Bs (I./StG 2) found the Fiats' 'campaign field', destroying 14 Falcos, completely annihilating one squadron (3/II/2).

Having escaped destruction at Schaffen, at midmorning the Fox fighters (5/III/2) took off from their 'campaign field' at Vissenaken and encountered two *Staffeln* of Bf 109Es (1./JG 1 and 3./JG 27) sweeping the area; eight Foxes were shot down or badly damaged. The following afternoon, Stuka attacks (StG 2) destroyed six of the survivors, annihilating the unit. The next day Groupe III (6/III/2) handed its nine surviving – and chronically obsolete –

One of only three combat squadrons to survive the Luftwaffe's opening air attacks, Escadrille 5/III/3 launched all nine of its serviceable Fairey Battles to attack three bridges spanning the Albert Canal. Attacking in the face of fierce fighter opposition and flak barrages, six of these light bombers were lost. (Daniel Brackx)

biplanes to 3eme Regiment at Aalter (near Ghent) and evacuated to Norrent-Fontes, France, to re-equip.

More Dorniers and escorting Messerschmitts struck Neerhespen at 0550hrs, just after 3eme Regiment's ancient Fox IIIC bomber biplanes (Groupe I) arrived, destroying eight and damaging six, all of which were abandoned in the ensuing retreat. At 0515hrs Heinkel He 111s (KG 27) hit the evacuated Brussels-Evere base, destroying another six Foxes – effectively eliminating the biplane bomber group – as well as three Fairey Battles (5/III/3) and a prototype LACAB GR8 transport-bomber.

Because the strike against Antwerp's Deurne airfield (KG 27) was the deepest penetration, it was escorted by 30 Bf 110C *Zerstörer* (ZG 26). By the time the raid arrived overhead, the local reconnaissance unit (1/I/1) had evacuated and, because the AéM's fighter force had been completely smothered by the Luftwaffe, to the German aircrews the uneventful mission 'seemed like a training flight'.

The first day's onslaught crippled the AéM, leaving only two fighter (Gladiators and CR.42s), one bomber (Battles), and three army cooperation/observation (Foxes and Renards) squadrons operational. The Luftwaffe's initial counter-air phase was an outstanding success, destroying 83 Belgian aircraft at 15 airfields. Unchallenged by the Allies, the invader had achieved aerial supremacy over central Belgium.

With the ground forces unable to prevent the capture of the Albert Canal bridges – or retake them – the next day, the AéM's two most capable units (5/III/3 Battles and 1/I/2 Gladiators) attempted to destroy them. At 0600hrs nine Battles, each lugging eight 110 lb (50kg) bombs, launched from Besele and were escorted by six Gladiators from Beauvechain. The escorts were stripped away by patrolling Messerschmitts (1./JG 1), which shot down four and damaged the other two, and two Battles were lost to others (1./JG 27) before braving the fierce flak (I./Flak-Rgt 'Göring' [mot.]) over the bridges. Attacking at low altitude through a maelstrom of fire, none of the bridges were hit and four more Battles fell in flames, the remaining three recovering, damaged, to Aalter.

Completing the destruction of the AéM's combat force, two afternoon strafing attacks by Messerschmitts (I./JG 1) destroyed the seven remaining Gladiators. The last Belgian fighter unit (6/II/2) was withdrawn to the north, to Nieuwkerke–Waas, and ordered to avoid contact with German fighters. Complete air dominance had been achieved.

The 'Matador's Cloak' unfurled: 10–11 May

The panzer's route onto the broad Belgian plain was through the magnificent ancient city of Maastricht. Situated in the small indefensible 'appendix' of Dutch Limburg, the local commander, Luitenant-Kolonel Albert Govers, had five companies of border troops, totalling 750 men, augmented with eight new Solothurn 20mm anti-tank rifles. Three companies were arrayed to the east, one covered the three bridges inside the city and the Borgharen sluice-gate north of town, and the fifth (reserve) faced Belgium.

In the pre-dawn darkness, before X-hour, German Army commandos of Bataillon zbV 100, dressed as Dutch police and riding bicycles, crossed the border attempting to secure the bridges in and north of Maastricht. These were followed by armoured cars, lorried troops and motorized flak guns from the same unit, trailed by Generalleutnant Joachim Stever's Aufklärungs-Abteilung (mot.) 7 (Aufkl.-Abt. [mot.] 7). The disguised commandos failed at every point, forcing the motorized detachments to engage the Dutch defenders, who fought back tenaciously, 47 of them dying at their street barricades. Between 0740 and 0800hrs the panzer's SdKfw 222/231 armoured cars arrived at the three bridges, only to watch helplessly as 'the Maastricht bridges [flew] into the air just under the nose of the 4. Panzer-Division'.

With his riverside defences compromised by motorized commandos taking the Borgharen sluice-gate and with only two companies remaining, Govers surrendered the city at 1100hrs. The Germans had lost 186 killed and nine armoured cars destroyed.

Stever's combat engineers (Pion.-Bat. [mot.] 79) immediately set to work building three replacement bridges, using the 8-tonne pontoons to ferry the lighter vehicles while completing two 4-tonne Brückengerät C personnel bridges by noon. The riflemen of Schützen Brigade (mot.) 10 (SB [mot.] 10) began crossing, collecting their vehicles on the west side and by early afternoon set off in force for the bridges spanning the Albert Canal. Schützen Regiment (mot.) 33 (SR [mot.] 33) headed west, crossing the Veldwezelt bridge while SR (mot.) 12 crossed the Vroenhoven bridge. Mid-afternoon, the motorized infantry relieved the paratroopers, took possession of their 670 prisoners and viciously attacked Major-General Eugène Van Trooyen's shocked and shattered 7eme Division d'Infanterie. Within 24 hours Stever's riflemen destroyed the Belgian unit – capturing another 6,637 prisoners – while the neighbouring 4eme Division, 'acknowledged to be the worst in the Belgian army', evaporated in mass desertions and surrenders. The 'door' into Belgium had been truly and completely 'kicked in'.

By 0430hrs the next morning (11 May) Stever's first tanks were ferried across the Maas and an hour later the 16-tonne Brückengerät B pontoon bridge was completed, allowing his Panzer Brigade (mot.) 5 (PzB [mot.] 5) to cross in strength. By midmorning the brigade's two regiments joined SB (mot.) 10 on the high ground west of the Albert Canal. Following immediately behind, Stumpff's 3. Panzer-Division took its position on Stever's right wing and at 1315hrs Hoepner took operational control, XVI AK (mot.) setting off towards Tongeren with the 20. Infanterie-Division trailing.

With the collapse of the Belgian Ière Corps and the failure of the AéM's early morning air attack, Allied air forces mounted a series of raids against the Maastricht and Albert Canal bridges and the armoured and motorized columns crossing them. Early morning reconnaissance by BEF (AC) Blenheim IVs (18 Sqn) only resulted in two aircraft shot down by flak.

With two of the three Albert Canal bridges near Maastricht secured, Hoepner's XVI AK (mot.) began crossing into Belgium the next day. In addition to Bunker N guarding the roadway from the far end of the Veldwezelt Bridge, Bunker C, built into the base of the bridge's support, covered the canal. (NARA)

Luftwaffe flak batteries were in the midst of the fighting at the Albert Canal. Driving forward on the first day, I./Flak-Rgt 'Göring' (mot.) provided direct fire support for the paratroopers holding the two bridges, helping to repulse Belgian counter-attacks. The next day they deployed around the bridges to fend off the Allies' air attacks. (Thomas Laemlein)

Later missions returned, damaged, with photos enabling Bomber Command to launch 23 Blenheim IVs late that afternoon, 21 Squadron attacking panzer columns on the Maastricht–Tongeren road and 110 Squadron bombing the pontoon bridges in Maastricht from medium altitude. Eight bombers attacking the panzers were badly damaged by flak while intercepting Messerschmitts (3./JG 27) shot down two over Maastricht. An hour later, 13 Groupement de Bombardement du Jour No 6 (GB I and II/12) LeO 451s, escorted by 18 Morane MS 406 fighters (GC II/6), arrived to bomb the Maastricht pontoon bridges and German troop concentrations, flak shooting down three and damaging nine.

The next morning Blenheims returned, nine unescorted AASF bombers (139 Sqn) attacking Stever's armoured columns – now driving into Tongeren – on the roads west of Maastricht at 0620hrs. Richthofen's JG 27 provided effective fighter cover with two squadrons (2./JG 1 and 3./JG 27) viciously attacking the British bombers, shooting down seven (15 crewmen killed or missing, two captured) and damaging one.

Belatedly realizing that the Veldwezelt and Vroenhoven bridges were the critical choke points (even though, by now, the entire XVI AK [mot.] had already crossed them), AASF commander Air Vice Marshal P. H. L. Playfair launched five Fairey Battles (12 Sqn) against them. In the first challenge to the Luftwaffe's air supremacy over Belgium, two BEF (AC) fighter squadrons (87 and 615 Sqns) swept in from the west while eight AASF Hurricanes (1 Sqn) escorted the Battles as they approached from the south-west at 0915hrs. Patrolling Bf 109Es (2./JG 27 and 2.[J]/LG 2) engaged the British fighters, shooting down five and damaging three for the loss of two, and then flamed a Battle before flak shot down the other four (six crewmen killed – two being posthumously awarded the Victoria Cross – and seven captured). The Veldwezelt bridge was reported slightly damaged by a 250 lb bomb.

Simultaneously, two dozen Bomber Command Blenheims (15 and 107 Sqns) attacked bridges and roads near Maastricht. Richthofen's fighters (1./JG 1 and 2./JG 27) continued to have a field day, shooting down ten and damaging four beyond repair. Early that afternoon the AdA sent its Groupement de Bombardement d'Assaut 18 (GBA I and II/54) – 18 new, fast Breguet 693 twin-engine assault aircraft – against Stever's panzers. Escaping fighter interception, ten were blasted from the sky by I./FlaK-Rgt 'Göring' (mot.)'s motorized flak batteries. While the Allies' repeated air raids – flown with immense courage and at great sacrifice – did little materiel damage, they disrupted Hoepner's westward progress, the XVI AK (mot.) war diary noting 'attacked by enemy bombers, causing considerable delays'.

Any delay was beneficial as far as the Allies were concerned. Gamelin's 'Plan D' hinged on the BEF's ability to get to the Dyle River and Blanchard's 1ère Armée 'plugging' the Gembloux Gap, initially with Prioux's mechanized Corps de Cavalerie. Alerted at 0745hrs on 10 May, Prioux's armoured cars, tanks,

AOK 6's invasion of Belgium, 10–13 May 1940.

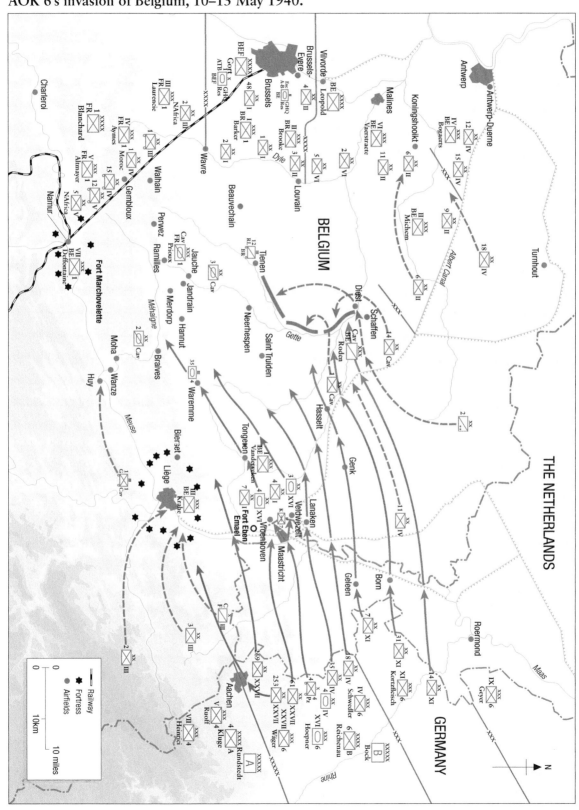

LEFT
RAF Battles attacking the bridges were no more successful, or fortunate, than the Belgians the day before – of five dispatched, four were lost to flak and the last to defending fighters. (Thomas Laemlein)

RIGHT
A French motorized anti-tank unit passing through a Belgian village, on the way to Gembloux. (IWM F4548)

lorried infantry, and towed artillery left Valenciennes (3e DLM) and Maubeuge (2e DLM), began crossing the Belgian border four hours later, followed that evening – due to the Luftwaffe's control of the Belgian skies, Blanchard ordered his main elements to travel only at night – by three motorized infantry (1er, 12e and 15e) divisions. Blanchard's remaining three infantry divisions (1er Moroccan, 2e and 5e North African) had to wait for their trains to be organized, arrive and be loaded, and they left the next day. Anxious to 'fill the gap' as quickly as possible, Prioux sent his reconnaissance regiments (8e and 12e Cuirassiers) racing ahead in four Détachements de Découverte ('discovery detachments'), their 80 Panhard 178 armoured cars fanning out across the open Belgian countryside, driving 180 miles (290km) the first day.

With Stukas (StG 77) attacking everything in their path, Hoepner's panzers reached Tongeren – the former HQ of Lieutenant-général Vanderveken's Ière Corps d'Armee – mid-afternoon on 11 May. As Stever's riflemen (SR [mot.] 33) dismounted to secure the town, Vanderveken and his staff evacuated, joining the remnants of his two shattered divisions streaming westwards. Lieutenant-général de Neve de Roden's Corps de Cavalerie (2e Division de Cavalerie, 1ère and 14e Divisions d'Infanterie) established a covering position along the Gette River from Diest to Tienen (Tirlemont in French), allowing them to escape Schwedler's pursuing IV AK.

Regrouping near Tongeren, Hoepner sent his motorized reconnaissance and motorcycle infantry battalions (Aufkl.-Abt. [mot.] 3 and 7 and Kradschützen-Bataillon 3) ranging ahead while his panzers deployed to advance in strength against the French mechanized cavalry, which was being constantly watched by roving Henschel Hs 126B observation aircraft (2.[H]/41). The two panzer divisions drove towards Hannut in battle array, forming four *Kampfgruppen* ('battle groups'), each composed of a panzer regiment leading a motorized rifle and an artillery battalion. The four regiments deployed their panzers in textbook 'advance and engage' formation: each with its two battalions line-abreast, each battalion's third company leading with its ten PzKpfw IIIs in front, followed by its six PzKpfw IVs, and the two light tank companies (24 PzKpfw I/IIs each) on the flanks. Covered by Richthofen's fighters (JG 27) and actively supported by his Stukas (StG 2), Hoepner's four *Kampfgruppen* drove south-westwards in an armoured *Kiel* ('wedge') six miles wide. (In a brief lapse in the Luftwaffe's aerial superiority, on three dramatic and portentous occasions RAF Hurricanes from 3, 87, and 607 Sqns got through to shoot down 11 Stukas from I. and II./StG 2, one Do 17M from Stab/StG 2, and three Hs 126B battlefield observation aircraft.)

Meanwhile, as Prioux's Panhards sparred with Hoeper's SdKfw 222/231s and withdrew to report, his two mechanized cavalry divisions passed Gembloux, advancing to Hannut, a town situated on a broad, low ridge 18 miles (29km) beyond the 'Dyle Line'. Here the Belgian plain forms an expansive undulating landscape dotted with small villages and scattered woods. Prioux deployed his two cavalry divisions in a thin screen across a 22-mile (35km)-wide front (for perspective, Blanchard was manning his 20.5 mile [33km] segment of the Dyle Line with six divisions) with Général de Brigade Gabriel Bougrain's 2e DLM spread south of Méhaigne creek to Huy and Général Jean-Léon-Albert Langlois's 3e DLM occupying a 10-mile (16km)-long line of small villages in an arc from Crehen (on the ridge just south of Hannut) northwards to Tienen.

On 11 May, Hoepner's two panzer divisions drove deep into central Belgium, slowing occasionally to allow their motorized rifle troops to clear the towns along the route of any Belgian defenders, especially anti-tank teams. (NARA)

The tank battles at Hannut and Gembloux: 12–15 May

As Hoepner's *Kampfgruppen* passed Waremme, they literally began to 'run out of gas', forcing many elements to halt. While the others paused to refuel – provisioned by shuttling Ju 52/3ms delivering 20,000 litres of gasoline – Oberstleutnant Heinrich Eberbach's PzR 35 continued south-west to Avennes and Braives where they clashed tentatively with 2e DLM deployed along Méhaigne creek. At 0920hrs Eberbach was ordered to secure Hannut and he sent his 5. Kompanie (24 PzKpfw I/IIs) to do so, but an hour later they came under flanking fire from Hotchkiss H39s (3e Esc/2e Cuirassiers) at Crehen. Immediately Eberbach dispatched the rest of II. Bataillon to assist.

The fighting quickly intensified as the panzers attempted to apply their 'exercise grounds' tactics to real combat, advancing directly across open terrain – not using the farm fields' undulations to mask their approaches – in the face of superior French 37mm and 47mm weapons to very short range before manoeuvring to the flanks. Very quickly, disabled and burning panzers littered the battlefield around Crehen. Eberbach fed the fight with I. Bataillon and, using radios to advantage, his more numerous panzers soon flowed around the village, closing from all sides. Around noon the French were driven out, the ten surviving H39s withdrawing to Thisnes while the infantry (truck-mounted dragoons from 11e Régiment de Dragons Portés or 11e RDP) retreated to Merdorp. While II. Bataillon secured Crehen, Eberbach led the other – now reinforced with a battalion of motorized riflemen – in attacking Thisnes, destroying another 13 Hotchkiss tanks (4e Esc/2e Cuirassiers).

From Merdorp, at 1730hrs, the dragoons and nine SOMUAs (1ère Esc/2e Cuirassiers) counter-attacked and in three hours of tough fighting, and at the cost of four S35s,

From Tongeren the 4. Panzer-Division drove towards Hannut, clashing with the advanced screen of Prioux's Cavalry Corps there. Here HQ platoon of PzR 35's 6. Kompanie – a mixture of PzKpfw Is, IIs, and IIIs – advance towards Braives to begin the three-day tank battle. (NARA)

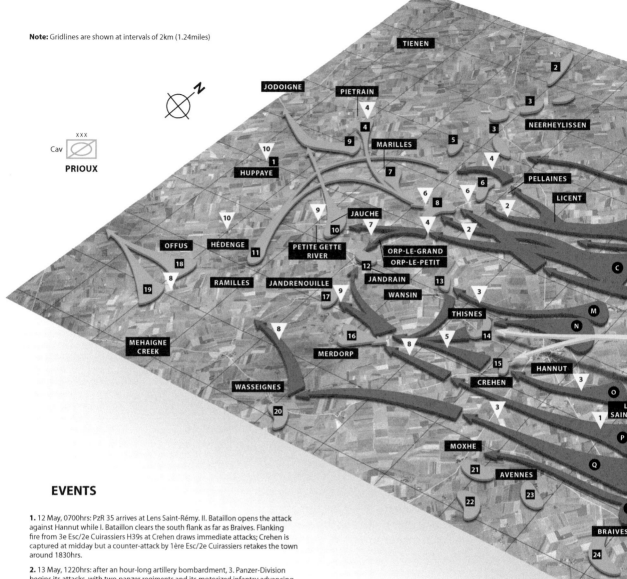

Note: Gridlines are shown at intervals of 2km (1.24miles)

Cav — **PRIOUX**

TIENEN

JODOIGNE

PIETRAIN

MARILLES

NEERHEYLISSEN

HUPPAYE

PELLAINES

LICENT

JAUCHE

OFFUS

HÉDENGE

PETITE GETTE RIVER

ORP-LE-GRAND
ORP-LE-PETIT

C

RAMILLES

JANDRENOUILLE

JANDRAIN

WANSIN

M

N

THISNES

MEHAIGNE CREEK

MERDORP

HANNUT

CREHEN

WASSEIGNES

SAIN

O
L

P

MOXHE

Q

AVENNES

BRAIVES

EVENTS

1. 12 May, 0700hrs: PzR 35 arrives at Lens Saint-Rémy. II. Bataillon opens the attack against Hannut while I. Bataillon clears the south flank as far as Braives. Flanking fire from 3e Esc/2e Cuirassiers H39s at Crehen draws immediate attacks; Crehen is captured at midday but a counter-attack by 1ère Esc/2e Cuirassiers retakes the town around 1830hrs.

2. 13 May, 1220hrs: after an hour-long artillery bombardment, 3. Panzer-Division begins its attacks, with two panzer regiments and its motorized infantry advancing to engage Ile/11e RDP at the villages along the Petite Gette River.

3. 1245hrs: following a half-hour Stuka bombardment, 4. Panzer-Division begins its assaults with Schützen-Brigade 4 (SB 4) securing the outposts at Wansin, Thisnes, and Crehen while its two panzer regiments drive west to engage the 2e Cuirassiers' S35s and surviving H39s at Merdorp.

4. 1330hrs: 3. Panzer-Division is halted at Orp-le-Grand, forcing Stumpff to concentrate his motorized riflemen and AT guns in a bitter contest to secure a bridgehead while, an hour later, to the north II./PzR 5 crosses the Petite Gette and begins to swing round behind the forward French units.

5. 1330hrs: having secured the outpost villages, SB 4 advances south-west to join PzR 35's assault on Merdorp. Supporting the defenders, 76e RATTT destroys or disables numerous vehicles as they approach Merdorp.

6. 1500hrs: Ile/11e RDP motorcyclists and H35s reinforce the infantry at Orp-le-Grand, while counter-attacks by 1ère Cuirassiers' H39s prevent II./PzR 5 from encircling the French frontlines. Fierce tank battles erupt for two hours.

7. 1520hrs: PzR 6 shifts towards Jauche, attempting to split 3e DLM, but is counter-attacked by 1ère Cuirassiers' S35s, resulting in another tank-vs-tank slugging match. Counter-attacks by 1ère Cuirassiers permit most of Ile/11e RDP to evacuate their forward positions along the Petit Gette.

8. 1600hrs: while PzR 35 and SB 4 are counter-attacked by 1ère Esc/2e Cuirassiers' S35s in another intense tank battle at Merdorp, PzR 36 sweeps around to the south, driving towards 76e RATTT at Ramilles. The French artillery withdraws – leaving the defenders at Merdorp unsupported.

9. 1800hrs: while III./SR 33 completes the capture of Merdorp, PzR 35 defeats 2e/2e Cuirassiers at Jandrenouille. Entering PzR 6's battle at Jauche by attacking Jandrain from the south, 3./PzR 35's PzKpfw IIIs and IVs finally break the French resistance – 3e DLM's subsequent retreat towards Jodoigne allows PzR 6 to cross the Petite Gette at Jauche at 1900hrs.

10. 1930hrs: PzRs 6 and 35 resume their advance, finally halting at Huppaye and Hédenge.

THE TANK BATTLE AT HANNUT, 12–13 MAY 1940

Attempting to drive to Gembloux to prevent the French Ière Armée from establishing a defensive line at Gembloux, the German 4. Panzer-Division began attacking the French Cavalry Corps (2e and 3e DLMs) at Hannut. The initial attacks were repulsed, but well-planned and well-coordinated attacks by both panzer divisions (3. and 4.) the next day eventually drove the 3e DLM from the field, causing a withdrawal to Gembloux.

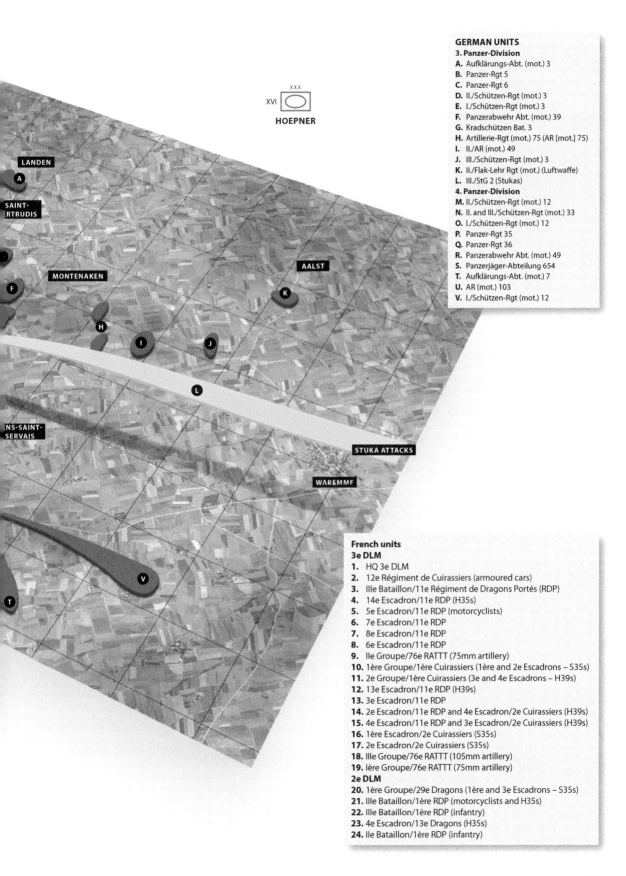

GERMAN UNITS

3. Panzer-Division
A. Aufklärungs-Abt. (mot.) 3
B. Panzer-Rgt 5
C. Panzer-Rgt 6
D. II./Schützen-Rgt (mot.) 3
E. I./Schützen-Rgt (mot.) 3
F. Panzerabwehr Abt. (mot.) 39
G. Kradschützen Bat. 3
H. Artillerie-Rgt (mot.) 75 (AR [mot.] 75)
I. II./AR (mot.) 49
J. III./Schützen-Rgt (mot.) 3
K. II./Flak-Lehr Rgt (mot.) (Luftwaffe)
L. III./StG 2 (Stukas)

4. Panzer-Division
M. II./Schützen-Rgt (mot.) 12
N. II. and III./Schützen-Rgt (mot.) 33
O. I./Schützen-Rgt (mot.) 12
P. Panzer-Rgt 35
Q. Panzer-Rgt 36
R. Panzerabwehr Abt. (mot.) 49
S. Panzerjäger-Abteilung 654
T. Aufklärungs-Abt. (mot.) 7
U. AR (mot.) 103
V. I./Schützen-Rgt (mot.) 12

XXX
XVI
HOEPNER

LANDEN

SAINT-RTRUDIS

MONTENAKEN

AALST

NS-SAINT-SERVAIS

STUKA ATTACKS

WAREMME

French units

3e DLM
1. HQ 3e DLM
2. 12e Régiment de Cuirassiers (armoured cars)
3. IIIe Bataillon/11e Régiment de Dragons Portés (RDP)
4. 14e Escadron/11e RDP (H35s)
5. 5e Escadron/11e RDP (motorcyclists)
6. 7e Escadron/11e RDP
7. 8e Escadron/11e RDP
8. 6e Escadron/11e RDP
9. IIe Groupe/76e RATTT (75mm artillery)
10. 1ère Groupe/1ère Cuirassiers (1ère and 2e Escadrons – S35s)
11. 2e Groupe/1ère Cuirassiers (3e and 4e Escadrons – H39s)
12. 13e Escadron/11e RDP (H39s)
13. 3e Escadron/11e RDP
14. 2e Escadron/11e RDP and 4e Escadron/2e Cuirassiers (H39s)
15. 4e Escadron/11e RDP and 3e Escadron/2e Cuirassiers (H39s)
16. 1ère Escadron/2e Cuirassiers (S35s)
17. 2e Escadron/2e Cuirassiers (S35s)
18. IIIe Groupe/76e RATTT (105mm artillery)
19. Ière Groupe/76e RATTT (75mm artillery)

2e DLM
20. 1ère Groupe/29e Dragons (1ère and 3e Escadrons – S35s)
21. IIIe Bataillon/1ère RDP (motorcyclists and H35s)
22. IIIe Bataillon/1ère RDP (infantry)
23. 4e Escadron/13e Dragons (H35s)
24. IIe Bataillon/1ère RDP (infantry)

recaptured Crehen, forcing Eberbach to disengage at Thisnes. At this point 'Der Alte Reiter' withdrew the battered PzR 35 and, deploying his other three (now replenished) panzer regiments on a narrow front north and south of Hannut, prepared for a renewed, concerted attack the next day.

Facing them, Langlois's division braced themselves for the next day's attacks, with two battalions of dragoons behind the Petite Gette, 2e Cuirassiers and one dragoon battalion (Ière/11e RDP) defending a string of hamlets west of Hannut, and his main armoured reserve – 87 S35s and H39s of 1ère Cuirassiers – waiting near Jauche, just behind the centre of his line. The rather ravaged 2e Cuirassiers and Ière/11e RDP – 40 H39s remained, with 38 S35s in reserve at Merdorp and Jandrenouille – would be confronted by Stever's somewhat depleted 4. Panzer-Division (36 PzKpfw IIIs, 20 PzKpfw IVs, and 200 PzKpfw I/IIs) while Stumpff's unblooded 3. Panzer-Division (42 PzKpfw IIIs, 26 PzKpfw IVs, and 240 PzKpfw I/IIs) assaulted the IIe/11e RDP along the Petite Gette. Throughout the day Bougrain's 2e DLM was occupied by four infantry columns (XXVII AK) that forced their way across the Méhaigne at Moha and Wanze, preventing him from supporting 3e DLM.

Supplementing Stever's artillery (AR [mot.] 103), while Stumpff's guns (AR [mot.] 75 and II./AR [mot.] 49) pounded French positions along the Petite Gette, Stukas (III./StG 2) delivered a 30-minute bombardment of Thisnes and Crehen. Hoepner's attacks began at 1230hrs with Stever's riflemen assaulting the two small hamlets – now only outposts – near Hannut while his panzers roared by to the south, headed for Merdorp and Wasseignes. In the north, however, fierce French resistance at Orp-le-Grand and Orp-le-Petit repulsed Stumpff's panzers and forced bitter infantry fighting to capture bridges across the Petite Gette.

Swinging round the dragoons' strongholds, PzR 5 crossed the stream in a gap between French defences while, at 1520hrs, PzR 6 angled southwards attempting to relieve pressure on the 4. Panzer-Division by driving to Jauche. Both were met with armoured counter-attacks and veritable *Hexenkessel* ('witches' cauldron') tank battles ensued.

At Merdorp – the key to Langlois's southern flank – Stever's PzR 35 and motorized riflemen were repulsed in heavy fighting, the Cuirassiers and dragoons supported by a tremendous artillery barrage, geysers of dirt and shrapnel erupting among the 250 panzers, damaging and disabling many of them. This spurred Eberbach to initially continue west with his panzers to overrun Langlois's exposed artillery (Ière and IIIe/76e RATTT), at which time the S35s (1ère Esc/2e Cuirassiers) sallied from Merdorp to maul the German riflemen, forcing his return. Eberbach then invested the town; while the SOMUAs' 47mm guns held the panzers at bay, his infantry infiltrated amongst the houses eliminating the defending dragoons and A/T crews. Mid-afternoon, the surviving tanks – ten S35s and two H39s – broke out to Jandrenouille.

Eberbach followed, attacking at 1715hrs with infantry and A/T guns (II./SR [mot.] 33 and Panzerjäger-Abteilung 654) and sending his heavy panzers and engineers (3./PzR 35 and Pion.-Bat. [mot.] 79) to attack Jandrain, taking some pressure off PzR 6's battle near Jauche by attacking from the rear. In another

Once secured, III./SR 33's motorized infantry, reinforced with a battery of Panzerabwehr-Abt (mot.) 49's 3.7cm PaK 36 A/T guns, deployed in the streets and buildings of Merdorp to defend it against the anticipated French counter-attacks. (Thomas Laemlein)

Hexenkessel the panzers finally broke the French resistance, destroying eight S35s and capturing five more (1ère Cuirassiers), as well as 400 troops and four A/T guns (Ière/11e RDP). His line pierced at Jauche-Jandrain, Prioux ordered a general retreat.

In the north, most of 1ère Cuirassiers and their supporting elements were able to disengage, leaving behind 26 destroyed, disabled, and abandoned tanks. In the south, 2e Cuirassiers and 11e RDP had again suffered heavily, losses now totalling 80 of their original 108 tanks, and dragoons were reduced to battalion strength. During the night Langlois withdrew his battered division to Prioux's intermediate stop line, approximately 5.5 miles (9km) ahead of Blanchard's *ligne principale de résistance* (main line of defence). Still fighting off German infantry, Bougrain's 2e DLM did not retreat until after dark.

Although retiring over refugee-clogged roads was difficult, by morning both divisions were positioned in a coherent defence behind the Belgian 'continuous A/T obstacle', essentially a serrated steel fence called *barrage de Cointet*, running from Beauvechain to Fort Marchovelette. Prioux was reinforced by 25 armoured cars and a battalion of motorcycle troops (4e GRDIm of 15e DIM), holding the centre of the line in the woods at Perwez.

Hoepner halted the pursuit at 2100hrs to laager at Huppaye (3. Panzer-Division) and Ramillies-Offus (4. Panzer-Division), moving out the next morning at 0600hrs. Aided by his Henschel spotter planes (4.[H]/13 [Pz]), in a four-hour bombardment Stever's artillery smashed the *barrage de Cointet* at Perwez, with his pioneers breaching the barrier at 1030hrs. The obstacle itself was unmanned; French positions in woods, ravines, and villages behind it taking the Germans under fire when they came through the gaps blown in the steel 'fence'.

Eberbach's PzR 35 penetrated the line and became embroiled in fierce fighting while PzR 36 was repulsed at Grand Leez then shifted north to follow Eberbach's panzers through the gaps at Perwez. On the north flank, Stumpff's PzR 6 was initially delayed but eventually breached the *barrage de Cointet*, making progress against stubborn resistance until midday when they were halted by tank-supported Moroccan infantry (Ière/7e RTM and 35e BCC) at Ernage, just north of Gembloux, losing five panzers to the Renault R35s and A/T guns. PzR 5 broke through at Thorembais but at Walhain was

THE TANK BATTLE AT HANNUT – DEFENDING JANDRAIN, 1420HRS, 13 MAY 1940 (PP. 72–73)

'I backed my tank and stopped under an apple tree. There I sat on the open turret door and observed through my field glasses the plain [ahead] … I saw an extraordinary show played out about three kilometres [two miles] away: a panzer division shaping itself for battle. The massive gathering of this armoured armada was an unforgettable sight', recalled Sous lieutenant Robert le Bel, a platoon commander in Capitaine Lizeray's 13e Escadron of the 11e RDP. 'Some men, probably officers, walked to and fro gesticulating in front of the tanks. They were probably giving last minute orders to the tank commanders, the head and shoulders of whom I could see between the open two parts of the turret hatches. Suddenly as if swept away by a giant stick, they all disappeared. No doubt H-hour was approaching … A dust cloud appeared on the skyline, disclosing the enemy move. I got down into the tank, closed the hatch and peered through the episcopes.'

Lizeray's score of Hotchkiss H39s, as well as most of Capitaine Laffargue's 1ère Batallion/11e RDP of mounted infantry ('dragoons') and a battery of four 25mm anti-tank guns (13e EDAC) were defending the Belgian village of Jandrain. The neighbouring village of Jauche was defended by the SOMUAs of the 1ère Cuirassiers and was the HQ of the sector commander, Lieutenant-Colonel de Vernejoul. Jandrain and Jauche formed the linchpin connecting the two wings of Général Langlois's defensive line.

The panzers began their advance at midday, first attacking Orp-le-Petit, the next village to the north, before shifting south; 2. Kompanie/PzR 6 – about 20 PzKpfw I/IIs accompanied by two PzKpfw IVs – attacked the northern outskirts of Jandrain an hour later. The defenders included Sous lieutenant Jolibois's **(1)** platoon of five H39s supported by the 3e Escadron of dragoons **(2)**, and a 25mm A/T gun **(3)**. Sergeant Morel's A/T gun crew quickly knocked out a PzKpfw I **(4)** and the remaining light tanks scurried off to the west **(5)**, leaving the heavier PzKpfw IVs **(6)** bombarding the French positions with 7.5cm cannon fire. Jolibois and five dragoons were killed.

By 1500hrs elements of II./PzR 6 arrived, PzKpfw IIIs engaging in a slugging contest that destroyed half of Lizeray's H39s as the panzers penetrated into the village from the north and west. Laffargue ordered Lizeray to withdraw his remaining H39s and form a 'last square' in the village centre. Battling tenaciously for another hour, with Hauptmann Ernst Freiherr von Jungenfeld's 6./ PzR 35 closing in from the south and engaging the SOMUAs at Jauche, de Vernejoul ordered Laffargue to withdraw his dragoons to the west. But with the village invested from three sides, and the fourth under constant fire, only le Bel – leading four other H39s – was able to escape.

According to the panzers' war diary, 'Fire was opened on every one of these moving tanks by PzR 6 and the PaK Kompanie, so that every tank took a large number of hits, including 7.5cm high-explosive rounds. None of the French tanks was penetrated and put out of action.' After the battle, le Bel's Hotchkiss showed impact marks from being hit by 15 A/T rounds and 42 bullets.

repulsed by 2e Cuirassiers' surviving SOMUAs, heavily supported by artillery (1ère RAD, 201e RALD and 106e RALH), before the French finally withdrew, leaving behind another ten destroyed or damaged S35s.

Having successfully fulfilled his mission of delaying Hoepner's panzers, that evening Prioux withdrew his two mechanized cavalry divisions through Blanchard's lines, having lost 40 SOMUAs and 94 Hotchkisses in the hard-fought three-day battle.

Their mission in Belgium complete, on 18 May Hoepner's panzers headed south-west, via Charleroi, to join Kluge's AOK 4 and the drive to the Channel coast. (Thomas Laemlein)

The next day Hoepner attempted to force his way through Ière Armée's positions north of Gembloux, but was unable to make a successful penetration. By the time his corps was withdrawn from the battle on 16 May, his two divisions had lost 48 tanks destroyed – 36 PzKpfw I/IIs, six PzKpfw IIIs and six PzKpfw IVs – but another 174 were unserviceable due to battle damage or mechanical breakdown.

Once Prioux's two divisions filtered through his front lines, Blanchard reverted to the infantry side of the French Army's schizophrenic tank doctrine, reassigning each tank battalion to one of his division and corps commanders as *colmatage* ('plugs') to counter local breakthroughs. While Prioux was bitterly disappointed, noting, 'They have already begun to dismember the Cavalry Corps and are distributing the tanks along the line,' Blanchard felt justified because, as of 12 May, he had been sent two heavy Divisions Cuirassée (1ère and 2e DCrs) with which to form his own armoured reserve. In motivating this assignment Hoepner, Reichenau, and Bock's aggressive offensive had fulfilled Heeresgruppe B's mission to 'divert to themselves the strongest possible Anglo-French forces'.

With Guderian's and Rommel's dual successes on the Meuse on 14 May Blanchard's two DCrs were hurriedly reassigned to Corap's shattered 9e Armée, but would be destroyed before they could make a difference: 1ère DCr by 5. Panzer-Division while refuelling near Dinant and 2e DCr by 6. Panzer-Division en route to Sedan. Four days later, Hoepner's XVI AK (mot.) was reassigned to Heeresgruppe A and headed south-west to join the panzers' headlong charge to the Channel coast and help encircle the Allied armies in Belgium.

The bitter retreat: 16–20 May

Except for the 'Breda extension', Gamelin's 'Dyle Plan' deployment proceeded with few disruptions. The precipitate collapse of the Belgian Ière Corps caused Blanchard to hurry his infantry forward, travelling even during daylight. Kesselring's Luftflotte 2 attempted to slow their progress by bombing train stations, railway lines, and major roads, but did not attack the many columns of the 1ère Armée and BEF. As the three British and six French divisions began arriving at their designated positions – and the Belgian Army withdrew to the K-W Line – it became obvious that a formal command structure was needed to coordinate, if not direct, the disparate elements of (now) three Allied armies.

On 12 May, French Defence Minister Édouard Daladier and Généraux Georges and Billotte travelled to Château Casteau, near Mons, to meet with King Léopold and General van Overstraeten, with Lieutenant-General Henry R. Pownall, Gort's COS, representing the BEF. Despite the unsettling reverses in southern Holland and on the Albert Canal, prospects for a successful defence in central Belgium seemed favourable, provided all parties were equally committed and a proper command structure could be established. Until this point, command arrangements were politically expedient but militarily unworkable. For example, Lord Gort, as the highest-ranking representative of HM's government, answered to Gamelin, while Général Giraud was under Georges, not Billotte's, direction. Now Léopold, at once both the Belgians' national leader and commander of their army, was added to the mix.

Since Gamelin abdicated all control of events (thus insulating himself from potential blame), Georges decided that Billotte should direct the Belgian Army and BEF in addition to placing a fourth French army (Giraud's) under his command. Billotte objected that such a broad span-of-control was beyond his staff's capabilities, but being the senior French general in the region, the others agreed that he should be the one 'to ensure that the operations of the Allied Armies in Belgium and Holland were co-ordinated'.

In the Allied centre, the BEF's deployment 'went remarkably smoothly', especially considering the lack of pre-campaign coordination. The 12th Royal Lancers ranged out ahead of the three forward divisions (1st, 2nd, and 3rd) with these arriving on the shallow wooded banks of the Dyle, deploying along a 17-mile (27km)-wide front from Louvain to Wavre on the evening of 12 May.

To Gort's left, behind a stout, inspired defence by Roden's Corps de Cavalerie on the Gette River, the Belgian infantry withdrew in good order to the 'K-W Line', manning a 31-mile (50km) front with eight divisions, backed up by three more, with another two on the Willebroek Canal and a reserve of cavalry and the 1ère Division ChA. By 14 May, on the northern flank Giraud's 7e Armée withdrew to defend the Scheldt Estuary.

On Gort's right, Blanchard's 1ère Armée deployed with a strong defence-in-depth supported by massed artillery. In one of the major 'disconnects' caused by the lack of pre-campaign coordination, the Belgians expected the French to advance and hold the line Wavre–Perwez–Namur and had built the *barrage de Cointet* accordingly, but Blanchard found this position untenable and instead elected to defend along the Wavre–Gembloux–Namur railroad because its embankments offered a stronger natural defence.

Retreat of the Allied armies, 16–21 May 1940.

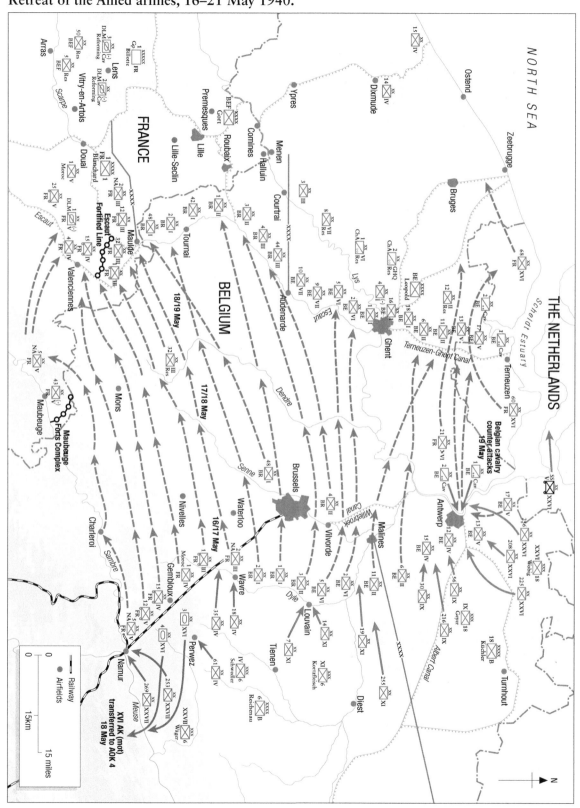

The south flank – originally manned by the Belgian IIIeme Corps (2eme and 3eme Divisions d'Infanterie) around Liège – withdrew to Namur, leaving the 12 forts to their fates. There they were joined by Groepering-K, arriving from the Ardennes, and reinforced by the French 12e DIM.

All told, the Allies had 22 divisions on the Dyle Line, with another 12 in reserve. They were faced with defending against Reichenau's AOK 6, which now numbered 16 infantry divisions. In the north Wobig's XXVI AK pushed Giraud's forward divisions back to Antwerp 'in disorder' while on the K-W Line, General der Infanterie Hermann Geyer's IX AK assaulted the Belgians' IVeme Corps. Astutely, Reichenau attempted to penetrate the Allied line at the 'seams' between its disparate armies. At Louvain Generalleutnant Joachim von Kortzfleisch's XI AK made contact with the BEF and attempted a breakthrough, unsuccessfully. General der Infanterie Viktor von Schwedler's IV AK attacked at Wavre, driving the French 3e Corps back to the Lasne River before Blanchard's reserves restored the line. Namur, the fortified southern anchor to the 'Dyle Line', held stoutly against assaults by General der Infanterie Alfred Wäger's XXVII AK.

But by this time, Billotte had much more to worry about than the conglomerate holding the Dyle Line. Aware from d'Astier's aerial reconnaissance that 'large motorized and armoured forces are driving toward the Meuse at Dinant, Givet, and Bouillon', initially the Groupe d'Armées 1 commander, like all the French Army generals from Gamelin down, did 'not believe that this is anything urgent, nor that the movement towards Sedan is the main effort'.

Twenty-four hours later Rommel had forced a crossing at Dinant, Kempf was assaulting Monthermé, and Guderian was across the Meuse at Sedan. The French high command reacted strongly, dispatching the three DCrs to 2e and 9e Armées, but the day was filled with disasters, with Corap's centre (11e Corps) being overrun by Rommel – the luckless French general ordered his forces to withdraw to the French frontier. To maintain the integrity of his front, Billotte recommended 9e Armée hold an 'intermediate stop-line' between Charleroi and Rethel. Accordingly, at 1900hrs Billotte ordered Blanchard to withdraw the 1ère Armée to the Charleroi Canal, connecting Tubize (near Waterloo) with the Sambre River.

Following a successful defence of Gembloux on 15 May, Blanchard ordered his army to retire that night so as to be in place along the Charleroi Canal by the morning of the 17th. The retreat was conducted in an orderly fashion, but its urgency caused much equipment, artillery, and A/T weapons to be abandoned, materiel that Blanchard could hardly afford to lose.

The excessive demands of coordinating the operations of six armies became all too apparent at this stage, when Billotte's overworked staff was finally able to devise a fighting retreat to the Escaut River and issue instructions to the BEF and Belgian Army the next morning. Groupe d'Armées 1 was to withdraw in three phases: to the Senne River on the night of 16/17 May, to the Dendre on 17/18, and the Escaut on 18/19 May.

Following closely after the retreating Allied armies, German infantry and artillery attempted to maintain contact with their withdrawing opponents. Passing an abandoned SOMUA tank, the pursuers – following on foot and on horses – could hardly keep pace. (Thomas Laemlein)

The BEF's withdrawal, if somewhat confused by conflicting information received from its flanks, was conducted in good order and 'was not vigorously pursued in its retreat to the Escaut'. Taking its positions between Audenarde and Maulde, by 21 May the BEF manned a strong defensive position, having 'suffered only about 500 battle casualties' thus far.

For the Belgians, the retreat was 'an especially bitter pill'. Having thrown their lot in with the Allies, now the greater part of the country – including Brussels, Antwerp, and Namur – was abandoned to the Germans. On the K-W Line, IVeme Corps held Geyer's IX AK while IIeme and VIeme Corps withdrew to the Willebroek Canal on 16 May, with all four corps retiring to the Dendre and Léopold's GHQ moving to Ghent the next day.

To replace Giraud's 7e Armée, which was being dismantled to provide forces for stemming the massive panzer breakthrough to the south, the Belgian Corps de Cavalerie (now consisting of the two cavalry divisions and the depleted tank squadron) regrouped just west of Antwerp. While Roden's cavalry mounted spirited counter-attacks led by their few light tanks, successfully checking XXVI AK's advances, Léopold's army withdrew in good order, deploying along the Escaut from Terneuzen to Audenarde. However, by this time, through all this effort, they were exhausted.

Giraud's 7e Armée was disbanded on 18 May, the remaining corps (16e Corps, three divisions under Général Alfred Fagalde) being attached to the Belgian Army. Billotte sent the 9e DIM to guard the Oise River between Hirson and Guise (where it was destroyed by 8. Panzer-Division) and the 1ère DLM and 25e DIM were dispatched to join the shattered 9e Armée. Three days prior Giraud replaced Corap, but the situation was beyond salvaging and by 18 May his new command was completely overrun, Giraud being captured the next day.

On 20 May the Allies' situation went from bad to worse when Guderian's panzers reached the Channel coast, sealing the three Allied armies in a boot-shaped pocket defined by Ghent, Dunkirk, and Lille. The day before Gamelin had been sacked, and 73-year-old Général d'Armée Maxime Weygand became the new Commandant Suprême des Armée Alliées. A breath of fresh air, Weygand had a plan to cut off the over-extended panzers and ordered the AdA to fly him to Calais, from where he would travel to Ypres to discuss his ideas with Billotte, Léopold, and Gort.

A change in the air: 15–21 May

Initially assigned to Luftflotte 2, Richthofen's Fliegerkorps VIII had been intended to support Reichenau's AOK 6 advance across Belgium until it was needed to help enable Gruppe Kleist's vault across the Meuse at Sedan and Monthermé. But the speed of Guderian's approach to Sedan surprised everyone and Stuka support was needed just as Hoepner's battle at Hannut escalated to full fury. Surprised by Jeschonnek's movement order, received late on 12 May, Richthofen was reluctant to cancel his commitments to Reichenau, so a compromise was reached whereby Richthofen's units and command elements were transferred piecemeal to Luftflotte 3.

Even after Richthofen's Stukas transferred south to support Kleist, IV.(St)/ LG 1 was retained to support AOK 6, moving to the former AéM airfield at Bierset and bombing forts around Liège and Namur, as well as Allied columns retreating to the Scheldt River. Likewise, Fiebig's KG 4 directly supported Küchner's AOK 18 as the victors from Holland took charge of IX and XXVI AKs attacking the Belgian Army as it withdrew to the Escaut. Meanwhile,

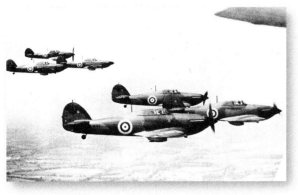

KG 54 augmented Keller's Fliegerkorps IV supporting Riechenau's continued pressure on – and pursuit of – the other retiring Allied armies. To facilitate these operations, I./KG 30's Ju 88As moved to Schiphol airfield on 18 May and LG 1 deployed to Nivelles five days later.

To replace the transferred units, on 17 May General der Flieger Ulrich Grauert's Fliegerkorps I was reassigned to Kesselring. These units (primarily KG 1 with He 111s and KG 76 with Do 17Zs) remained at their pre-campaign bases east of the Rhine but adjusted their 'area of operations' to target the French 1ère Armée, supporting Generaloberst Günther Hans Kluge's AOK 4 against the south side of the Lille–Dunkirk pocket.

Battling these bombers, Allied air power underwent changes of its own. Reinforced by three Hurricane squadrons (3, 79, and 504 Sqns) and a group of Hawks (GC I/4), the BEF (AC) and AdA challenged Luftflotte 2's Messerschmitts in a lopsided battle of attrition. In the first six days of the campaign, Messerschmitts destroyed 30 Hurricanes, 22 Moranes, and five Hawks over Belgium, for the loss of nine Bf 109Es and two Bf 110Cs, a 'kill ratio' of over 5:1 (five 'victories' for each loss).

Despite assurances given by the War Cabinet following the impassioned and compelling (now famous) appeal by Air Chief Marshal Hugh Dowding, head of Fighter Command, Churchill still required the RAF to dispatch to France an additional 'ten fighter squadrons'. This was done, first, by sending eight flights (half-squadrons) to reinforce the BEF (AC)'s Hurricane units beginning 16 May. The next day these were supplemented by three complete and three 'composite' squadrons (composed of disparate flights) operating from Kent, flying missions over northern France in the morning, refuelling, and launching on a second sortie, then recovering to England for the night. (The complete units were 17, 32, and 151 Squadrons. Nos 56, 111, 213, 253, and 601 Squadrons each contributed both component flights to the two phases of this programme.)

The results – as Dowding predicted – were disastrous. By 21 May, when the approaching panzers forced Air Vice Marshal Blount's BEF (AC) to evacuate from France, the RAF had lost 195 Hurricanes, including 74 destroyed in aerial combat. From this point on, Fighter Command's badly depleted 11 Group would attempt to challenge the Luftwaffe's aerial superiority over the Flanders coastline from its airfields in Kent.

The road to Dunkirk: 21–28 May
Briefed on the current – as little as was known anyway – situation on 19–20 May, Maxime Weygand, weary from his gruelling flight from Syria, told

The final stand – escape to Dunkirk, 26–28 May 1940.

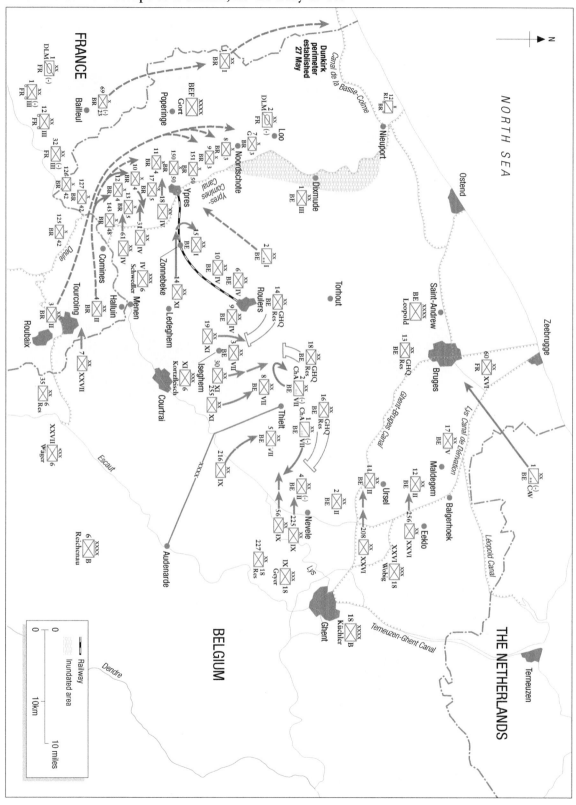

French Prime Minister Paul Reynaud, 'You will not be surprised if I cannot answer for victory, nor even give you the hope of victory … If I had known the situation was so bad I would not have come.'

Nevertheless, Weygand accepted the 'heavy responsibility' of commanding the Allied forces and at 1000hrs the following morning boarded a new, fast Amiot 354 twin-engine bomber at Le Bourget airport and, accompanied by another Amoit (GB II/34) and escorted by eight MB. 152s (GC II/3), he took off and flew north to meet the commanders of the three Allied armies now trapped in Belgium and northern France. Refuelling at the abandoned (former RAF) airfield at Norrent-Fontes, the formation flew on to Calais and Weygand travelled by car – a 'tortuous journey along roads clogged with army transport and refugees' – to Ypres for the first of three meetings.

First, at 1600hrs Weygand met with King Léopold and General van Overstraeten – with their French and British military liaisons in attendance – to outline his plan to cut off Heeresgruppe A's seemingly reckless thrust to the coast. The 'panzer corridor' was only 25 miles (40km) wide between Arras and the Somme River and it could be severed if powerful simultaneous attacks were launched in two days' time, before the lagging infantry divisions had time to 'close up' and secure the flanks of the corridor. These attacks were to be conducted, from the north, by the BEF and 1ère Armée and from the south by the newly reconstituted 7e Armée under Général Aubert Frère. The northern arm would consist of four French and three BEF divisions, but in order for Gort to participate, Léopold would have to withdraw his battered and exhausted forces to the Yser River, shortening the Allied defensive line facing Heeresgruppe B. The Belgians objected strenuously, Overstraeten stating that yet another retreat would be catastrophically demoralizing, emphasizing that 'the divisions are beginning to disintegrate under this succession of night retreats – the bane of discipline'.

The second meeting began when Générals Billotte and Fagalde arrived. After hearing Weygand's presentation, Billotte objected as well, saying that the 1ère Armée was in a confused situation and incapable of launching any counter-attacks. Consequently, Weygand proposed a compromise whereby, rather than withdrawing, the Belgians would extend their current front to the west, releasing three BEF divisions for offensive action.

The BEF's infantry was augmented with six battalions of 'divisional cavalry' comprising Vickers Mark VIb tankettes and 'Bren Gun Carriers'. Used in counter-attacks, especially along the Escaut, these lightly armoured, machine gun-armed units suffered heavy casualties. (IWM O681)

That day Gort was monitoring Major-General Giffard le Q. Martel's 'spoiling attack' to keep Rommel from taking Arras, enduring Bock's first serious and sometimes successful assaults against BEF units defending along the Escaut, sending auxiliary and support units (23,128 'useless mouths') to the Channel ports, and coordinating for a possible retreat to Dunkirk. Consequently, he remained in his command post (CP) at Prémesques, informed of Weygand's visit but not of its location. At Ypres, the frustrated Allied Supreme Commander waited until around 1830hrs before heading to Dunkirk to depart for Cherbourg aboard the French destroyer *Flore*.

The third meeting took place at 2100hrs, at Ypres, after Gort and Pownall were fetched from their CP. Chaired by Billotte, Léopold agreed to withdraw to the Lys to release one BEF division, Billotte would order Blanchard to extend his line north to free two more, and Gort would mount a counter-attack to the south in five days (26 May) with three divisions in concert with three French ones on his left flank. Tragically, that night, while returning to his CP at Lens to issue orders to Blanchard, Billotte was fatally injured in an automobile accident, and died two days later. Since no French officers were with him at the third meeting and Billotte carried no notes concerning the agreements, Blanchard visited Gort the next day to learn his army's role in the proposed plan to 'break out' to the south.

By this time Gort, Pownall, and other British generals were beginning to mistrust the Belgians, being convinced that Léopold could capitulate at any time, and each day were losing more confidence in the French High Command, forcing Gort to become more assertive in the direction of his own army. With seven divisions holding 30 miles (50km) of the Escaut Line and the 5th and 50th divisions dispatched to Vimy Ridge for the spoiling attack at Arras, Gort had every one of his frontline units committed to battle. Lacking an Allied leader (Billotte's successor was not appointed until 25 May) and with only a notion of a plan, the British and Belgian armies withdrew from the Escaut on the evening of 22/23 May. Four British divisions (1st, 3rd, 4th, and 42nd) retreated to the French frontier, manning pre-campaign fortifications from Maulde to Halluin, where the new Belgian line – manned by 13 exhausted divisions – turned right 90 degrees to follow the Lys from Menen (across the river from Halluin) to Ghent.

With both wings retiring, gaps naturally appeared between the two forces and, with the Luftwaffe's uninterrupted aerial reconnaissance, Bock was quick to recognize these and concentrated vicious attacks against this increasingly vulnerable seam. While Küchler's AOK 18 attacked the Belgian left flank on the Terneuzen Canal, forcing Roden's Corps de Cavalerie and the Veme Corps back from Ghent, Reichenau's XI AK (Kortzfleisch) and XXVII AK (Wäger) pressured the bulk of the Belgian and British armies, respectively. Between them Schwedler's IV AK forced its way across the Lys on both sides of Courtrai with four divisions, driving the Belgian 1ère and 3eme Divisions back toward Roulers, severing the link with the BEF.

Meanwhile, on 23 May Guderian's XIX AK (mot.) invested Boulogne and Calais, Reinhardt's XLI AK (mot.) rolled up to the string of canals stretching from Saint-Omer to Béthune, and Hoth's XV AK (mot.) forced Gort to abandon Arras. With seven panzer divisions in his rear areas, Gort hastily

LEFT
Once Bock's infantry caught up with the Allied armies, the battles devolved into traditional artillery slugging contests and infantry attacks. The Germans' superior modern artillery, such as the 10cm sK18 (seen here) and 10.5cm leFH 18, outranged the 'French 75', and were more accurate and had higher firing rates than the British and Belgian World War I-era weapons. (NARA)

RIGHT
Although the Allies attempted to hold the German advance from behind a series of contiguous 'water barriers', in fact most of these were easily fordable and were frequently infiltrated and penetrated by Bock's infantry. (NARA)

THE 3RD GRENADIER GUARDS COUNTER-ATTACK, 2000HRS, 27 MAY 1940 (PP. 84–85)

'The whole battalion moved past my headquarters. The setting sun was shining on their bayonets. Their Bren gun carriers were on either flank. In all my life I have never seen a finer and more awe-inspiring sight. They walked through the guns, and the men on them cheered as they passed.' Thus wrote Lieutenant-Colonel Franklin Lushington, 97th (Kent Yeomanry) Artillery Regiment R.A.

Pulling back from the French frontier defences at Roubaix the day before, the battalions of Major-General Harold Alexander's 1st Division were ordered to march to Dunkirk where they would be the first to man the port's perimeter. The retreat corridor was held open by Major-General Harold Franklyn's 5th Division, with the 143rd Brigade attached. Filling in behind the battered Belgian Army, which was forced to withdraw northwards from the Lys River, the 143rd Brigade deployed along the nearly dry Ypres Canal north of Comines with two 5th Division brigades extending the line to Ypres. Attacked violently throughout the day by the German 61. Infanterie-Division, these Territorials gave ground grudgingly, suffering heavy casualties, prompting Lieutenant-General Alan Brooke, commanding II Corps, to detach three 1st Division battalions to help stiffen the defence of the retreat corridor.

Despite having marched 20 miles during the night, Major Allan Adair led the tired Tommies of the 3rd Battalion The Grenadier Guards to the Bois de Ploegsteert where he received his orders – counter-attack eastwards until reaching the Comines–Ypres Canal – directly from Franklyn. After a brief rest, that afternoon Adair deployed his battalion in two ranks of two companies, line abreast with a section of Vickers Universal machine gun carriers on each flank and – with the 2nd North Staffordshires similarly arrayed on their left – advanced eastwards with fixed bayonets.

With the sun at their backs and a stout defence before them, the guardsmen began their attack just after 2000hrs, supported by barrages from five artillery regiments. However, soon they were subjected to heavy artillery and mortar fire themselves and were slowed by the cumbersome crossing of a deep, five-foot wide stream and 'innumerable fences'. The battalion's carrier platoon (1) engaged enemy machine gun nests concealed in a copse of trees – 'the whole front was lit up by the enemy's tracer ammunition' – while there was 'a farm blazing directly in front of ... 2 Company's line of advance' (2). As the dusk twilight faded into darkness, Major Adair (3) followed with 3 and 4 Company; 'the leading sections were silhouetted in the flames as they went forward towards the canal bank'.

By the time 1 and 2 companies reached the canal, they had suffered such horrendous casualties they were unable to hold the line and fell back a quarter of a mile to where 3 and 4 companies had dug in – using their bayonets as picks and shovels – in a long field ditch. The battalion held out against German shelling and attacks through the night and all the next day. At 2200hrs Adair and the survivors of the 3rd Grenadier Guards – only nine officers and 270 other ranks remained from the estimated 412 men that began the assault – made an orderly withdrawal towards Dunkirk.

deployed the three divisions (2nd, 44th, and 48th) freed by the most recent withdrawal, parcelling out their various brigades to man the 'Canal Line' and defend scattered 'stops' between La Bassée and Wormhoudt. (During World War II a British infantry brigade was the combat equivalent of a French or German regiment; a British regiment was the source organization for the battalions assigned to combat formations.) This left Gort with only two divisions (the 5th and 50th, called 'Frankforce' after the overall commander Major-General Harold E. Franklyn) with which to launch his part of the southward counter-attack. Blanchard was to contribute 2e and 5e Divisions d'Infanterie Nord-Africaine and 25e DIM – with the flanks covered by the reconstituted Corps de Cavalerie (now commanded by Langlois) which now mustered 75 operational tanks.

Meanwhile, the southern arm of Weygand's plan never crossed the Somme. Général Frère's first task was to take the bridgeheads from List's (AOK 12) motorized infantry and, on 24 May, two mixed horse/mechanized cavalry light divisions (2e and 5e DLCs) and Major-General Roger Evans' incomplete 1st Armoured Division attempted to do so but were repulsed. Consequently Frère cancelled his branch of Weygand's plan. Learning that day that Gort had abandoned Arras (envisaged as the springboard for the BEF branch of the offensive) Weygand informed Blanchard, 'if this withdrawal makes the operations as ordered impossible to carry out, try to form as big a bridgehead as possible covering Dunkerque, which is indispensable for administering further operations'.

Heeeresgruppe B was not affected by Hitler's controversial *Haltbefehl* ('halt order') so the next morning – after a day of heavy bombing attacks by Keller's Fliegerkorps IV, Fiebig's KG 4 and IV.(St)/LG 1's Stukas – Kortzfleisch's XI AK forced the Belgian VIIeme Corps back to Roulers and Thielt, and Schwedler's IV AK drove back the Belgian right wing (IVeme Corps). In heavy fighting German attacks opened an eight-mile (13km)-wide breach, advancing three divisions towards Ypres, headed towards Dunkirk. Informed that the southern branch of Weygand's plan was cancelled, Gort realized that, alone, its northern branch now stood no chance of success and, abandoning that plan, decided instead that the more desperate need was for Frankforce to fill the widening gap from the Lys to Ypres and planned to withdraw the rest of the BEF behind them. Blanchard concurred and dispatched 2e DLM (21 S35s and 18 H35/39s) to extend the Allied line north of Ypres. Agreeing with Gort that the only feasible response was to fall back on Dunkirk, at 1230hrs on 26 May he issued the order: 'the 1ère Armée, the BEF and Belgian Army will re-group progressively behind the water-line demarcated by the Aa Canal, the Lys [River] and Canal de Dérivation, in such a manner as to form a bridgehead covering Dunkirk in depth'.

Amidst the pervasive atmosphere of suspicion, mistrust, and posturing to avoid recriminations, while BEF planning for the withdrawal to Dunkirk naturally (to the British) included preparations for embarkation, Gort did not inform either of his two allies of this aim. At midday on 26 May, Gort received a message from Secretary of State for War Anthony Eden authorizing him to 'fight your way back to the west where all beaches and ports east of Gravelines will be used for embarkation,' following the next day with 'your sole task now is to evacuate to England maximum of your forces possible'.

If things had become desperate for the BEF, they were in extremis for the Belgians. Léopold's army was being bent into a separate pocket. Pushed back from the Lys, in the centre three tired corps (IIeme, VIeme, and VIIeme) held the line Roulers–Thielt–Nevele against incessant attacks by the German IX and XI AKs while the Cavalerie and Veme Corps defending the Lys Canal de Dérivation against Wobig's XXVI AK. Léopold's last reserve – Vanderveken's reconstituted Ière Corps (2eme Division de Cavalerie and 15eme Division d'Infanterie) – was rushed to the right flank and attempted to hold along the railroad line from Ypres to Roulers.

Separated from the BEF, physically spent and without further reserves, and with no means of following the Allies to Dunkirk, by the end of 25 May Léopold realized that his army's situation was now hopeless. The next morning XXVI AK assaulted across the Canal de Dérivation at Ronsele and Balgerhoeck and Geyer's IX AK engaged in a bitter battle for Nevele. In the centre, XI AK opened a four-mile (6.5km) gap between Thielt and Izegem, counter-attacks were repulsed and the Germans' route to Bruges and Ostend lay open.

At 1330hrs Léopold telegraphed Lord Gort: 'The time is rapidly approaching when [we] will be unable to continue the fight. [I] will be forced to capitulate to avoid a collapse.' An hour later Général Pierre Champon, the French liaison to the Belgian GHQ, was informed, 'the Army has reached the limits of its endurance' and, 'Belgian resistance is at its last extremity, our front is about to break.' With their backs to the sea, ammunition exhausted, and the hospitals overflowing, the Belgians had done all they could. At 1800hrs Léopold opened negotiations for the surrender of his army and his nation. Shortly before midnight the king accepted Hitler's demand for unconditional capitulation and a ceasefire went into effect at 0500hrs the next morning.

Later that day Reichenau and Major-Général Jules Derousseaux, representing King Léopold, signed the formal surrender document. To paraphrase Winston Churchill, 'the Battle of Belgium was over. The Battle of Dunkirk was about to begin.'

After 17 days of hard fighting, the Belgian surrender came into effect at 0500hrs on 28 May. (NARA)

AFTERMATH

A people which neglects its defence puts its freedom at risk.

Dutch historian Dr Louis de Jong, monument inscription at Rijsoord, 1975

In 18 days of continuous, intense combat Fedor von Bock's Heeresgruppe B conquered two small neutral nations and had convincingly baited the trap that, when it sprang, effectively isolated the two most powerful Allied armies. In doing so, the Luftwaffe had attempted the first-ever airborne *coup de main* (and failed) and had successfully seized the bridges in Holland and Belgium that enabled the panzers to race swiftly and deeply into the countryside.

Isolated as they were, there was nothing the Dutch could do except fight tenaciously with what little they had and, finally, when horribly confronted by the terrors of total war – against which they had no defence – they were compelled to surrender to the invaders. In Belgium the swift panzer advance resulted in the first great tank battle of the war, a three-day-long clash of modern armoured fighting vehicles in which German doctrine, mobility, flexibility, command and communications overcame superior French armour and armament. According to one noted historian, 'Gembloux was the hardest fought and most savage battle of the entire [*Fall Gelb*] campaign'.

Victory in the 12–14 May tank battles between Hannut and Gembloux has been given by historians to either side, depending on the author's allegiance. In fact, naming the victor should be made not on losses incurred but by aims or objectives achieved. At the tactical level, Hoepner's panzers proved victorious by mauling Prioux's 3e DLM and forcing a series of retreats that left the Germans in possession of the battlefields (and the ability to repair their disabled vehicles). At the operational (campaign) level, Prioux was successful in delaying the panzers' advance for three days, successfully allowing Blanchard to establish a solid defensive line that repulsed Hoepner's attempts to break it. At the strategic level, Reichenau's deep, swift penetration to Gembloux and the massive tank battle there achieved precisely the purpose Halder had envisaged for Heeresgruppe B and AOK 6: attracting 'the largest possible forces of the Anglo-French army' into Belgium, resulting in their isolation by Rundstedt's Heeresgruppe A and eventual destruction (French 1ère Armée) or evacuation (BEF), thus enabling *Fall Gelb*'s sequel – *Fall Rot* – to conquer France.

After driving from near Dunkirk through Antwerp and into southern Holland, and then retreating repeatedly from one defensive line to another, this battered Panhard AMD 178 finally returned three weeks later to where its journey began. (Thomas Laemlein)

Rotterdam after the 'clean up' of rubble following the devastating Luftwaffe bombardment on 14 May 1940. (DVIC HD-SN 99-02993)

On 26 May, eight hours after Eden authorized Gort to begin evacuating the BEF, the Admiralty ordered Dover Command to commence Operation *Dynamo* 'with the greatest vigour'. In one of the epic achievements in military history, 693 British vessels – supplemented by 168 French, Belgian, and Dutch – evacuated from Dunkirk and its nearby beaches some 357,362 Allied troops, finally ending at sunrise on 4 June. While almost all of the able-bodied French troops were cycled back to France via Southampton/Plymouth and Brest/ Cherbourg, the 221,504 British troops – plus another 144,171 brought home by Operations *Aerial* and *Cycle* and nearly 100,000 more evacuated from Norway – were gathered into six large military camps in the south of England, where they were organized into 24 divisions and prepared to defend against Hitler's anticipated invasion.

However, most of the 'Tommies' returned with only their rifles; almost all of the BEF's heavy weapons – tanks, artillery, A/T guns, and machine guns – had to be left behind. In a strange way this proved to be an advantage because at the time British tanks were pathetically inadequate and their artillery was almost entirely obsolete World War I leftovers. The massive losses forced Churchill to appeal to US President Franklin D. Roosevelt for the loan/lease of more modern military equipment. Though they temporarily lacked hardware, Britain had recovered the core of its professional army and upon this cadre would build a new army that would eventually, along with their Allies, emerge victorious over Hitler and his Wehrmacht.

For the time being, however, striking back through the air was the only means available to the British. Originally restrained because of fear of retribution in kind by the Luftwaffe, KG 54's bombing of Rotterdam, which killed 814 civilians, provided tacit permission for the RAF to retaliate by initiating their own attacks against German cities. Since Bomber Command was limited – due to the lethal effectiveness of the Luftwaffe's day fighter defence – to night bombing and because accuracy was unachievable with the relatively primitive technology and equipment of the day, the result was an eventually massive 'strategic bombing' campaign of German cities with no concern for civilian casualties.

While the Dutch consider the Rotterdam strike a 'terrorist act', it is important to note that, at the Nuremberg War Crimes Trials following the ultimate Allied victory in 1945, neither Göring nor Kesselring were indicted for the killing of civilians by the air raid on Rotterdam. On the other hand, if these two Luftwaffe leaders had been indicted for the Rotterdam attack, then would not the Allies' International Military Tribunal have been compelled to also consider indicting Marshal of the Royal Air Force Arthur 'Bomber' Harris, GCB, OBE, AFC, for his subsequent five-year night bombing campaign that destroyed numerous German cities, killing an estimated 600,000 German civilians?

THE BATTLEFIELD TODAY

To fully appreciate the enormity and difficulty of the task facing generals Hoepner, Stevers, and Stumpff, it is best to begin any exploration of the Hannut/Gembloux battlefields at Maastricht, on the right (east) bank of the Maas River. The Wilhelmina Bridge remains much as it was in 1940, only with the great hinged 'trap-door' section of the roadway fully in place instead of angling into the water (see the photo on page 52). Once across the Maas, the next obstacle is the wide Albert Canal, now spanned by a new, very modern bridge at Vroenhoven. As a memorial to the men who were lost here, the builders left the battle-scarred bunker on the bridge's western abutment intact, in recognition that – as its inscription declares – 'At this very place on the Albert Canal, World War II started for Belgium.'

Following the panzers' route via Tongeren and Waremme, it is remarkable what great 'tank country' the Hannut–Gembloux plateau really is: gently rolling countryside with flowing undulations ideal for mechanized manoeuvring with many high points crowned with small woods making excellent sites for anti-tank ambushes. The expansive plain is riven with small streams in narrow, but deep, valleys, invariably forested. Except for Hannut, Crehen, and Merdorp along the crest of the broad ridge, most of the villages – and they remain today much as they were in 1940 – are tucked into these ravines, great for concealing French armour until sallying out for a counter-attack, but limiting their fields of fire from defensive positions.

Not to be missed is the Musée du Corps de Cavalerie Français 1940, located in Jandrain, the site of an epic last-ditch defence before Prioux's line was finally breached. Housed in the former village schoolhouse and meeting hall – the CP of 11e RDP's Capitaine Laffargue during the battle – this small but excellent museum contains a large collection of artifacts and has detailed records of the battle, an invaluable treasure to any military historian researching the battle. Museum staff member Major Richard de Hennin offers battlefield tours, in English, to those that coordinate ahead of time (email curator Robert Van Dorpe at robert.vandorpe@gmail.com). This is good because, unlike the battlefields around Stonne, there are no monuments or memorials commemorating what occurred here in 1940.

The concrete bridge at Vroenhoven has been replaced by a modern steel structure, but the World War II bunker – with all its battle scars – remains today. (Author's collection)

The sole vestige for the ferocious tank battle at Hannut is the prominent water tower alongside the road between Jandrain and Jandrenouille. Impact marks from 2cm and 3.7cm rounds, as well as rifle and machine gun bullets, are plainly evident. (Author's collection)

The monument and memorial to the French Cavalry Corps at Jandrain. (Musée du Corps de Cavalerie Français)

The only remaining vestige of the battle is the famous water tower located on the high ground between Jandrain and Jandrenouille – both an artillery observation post for the French and a very visible *guidon*, a geographic objective used by the attacking panzer units. Plainly evident are the impact marks of 37mm shells and a volley of 20mm cannon fire, as well as numerous pocks made by rifles and machine guns. From this dominating position, the entire battlefield of 13 May can be viewed – noting the nearness of the neighbouring villages makes it easy to visualize how crowded this relatively small (6 mile/10km-square) battlefield was, with 256 German and 165 French tanks manoeuvring and fighting upon it. While in the area, visiting the Musée de la Ligne KW at Chaumont and Musée de la 1ère Armée Français at Cortil-Noirmont is also recommended.

In contrast to the rather unspoiled (but unmarked) battlefield around Jandrain, the route of 9. Panzer-Division across the Maas and through Mill to Moerdijk is largely lost in the expansive and unrelenting growth of modern civilization. At Moerdijk, on the south side one battlescarred *VIS-kazemat* (MG casemate) remains, while on the northern bank a large *B-kazemat* (river casemate housing an A/T gun), a *VIS-kazemat*, and several Pyramide group bomb shelters can be examined. The original 1936 steel truss highway bridge has been replaced with the A16's dual four-lane concrete spans, the former's long trusses being used to build the A27 motorway across the Bergse Maas, 12 miles (20km) to the east. Off the A16, one can see the bridges at Dordrecht much as they were in May 1940.

At Rotterdam, Waalhaven aerodrome has succumbed to suburbia, the Willemsbrug was replaced with a new one in 1981, and the razed inner city has been rebuilt with little likeness to its 1940 state. Most historically important, six miles (10km) south, at Rijsoord, the school that was once Student's CP is now the De Poort Institute where a large bronze plaque commemorates the inglorious day of the Dutch capitulation.

In fact, the only significant site remaining from the Dutch five-day war is the Grebbeberg, which – though heavily wooded now – is preserved so that visitors can see defensive bunkers and reconstructed trenches as they walk up the fairly steep slope from the ancient Hoornwerk bastion to the crest. Atop the hill is the Militair Ereveld Grebbeberg ('Grebbeberg Military Cemetary') where some 800 Dutch and German soldiers are buried. Although less strategically significant, at the east end of the Afsluitdijk, Fort Kornwerderzand is almost completely preserved and makes an excellent 'time capsule' to take one back to May 1940.

FURTHER READING

Surprisingly, for all the intensity, drama, sacrifice, and decisive results of Heeresgruppe B's conquest of Holland and Belgium, very little literature on these campaigns exists in English.

While there is ample coverage of their valiant defence by the Dutch in their own language, they are – partly because of the embarrassment of being so quickly overrun – reticent to share their experience with others. The best English-language source on the subject is Allert Goossens' 'War Over Holland, May 1940: The Dutch Struggle' (www.waroverholland.nl) – although the translation is somewhat rough and there is an understandably strong bias, this account is rich in detail and constitutes a comprehensive chronology of the campaign. Lt Kol E. H. Brongers' *The Battle for The Hague, 1940* (Uitgeverij Aspekt B.V.: Soesterberg, NL, 2004) – although more of a 'popular history' and limited to only its subject – is also recommended.

Largely eclipsed by the far more significant (but much less tank-vs-tank) battles at Sedan and Dinant, the epic armoured clash at Hannut is also 'under-reported' in English. There are no decent or accurate histories addressing it. The only acceptable account is Jeffrey A. Gunsburg's 'The Battle on the Belgian Plain, 12–14 May 1940: The First Great Tank Battle' published in *The Journal of Military History* (April 1992), but it contains inaccuracies and inappropriately assesses Prioux's performance against the blueprint of peacetime doctrine rather than the reality of the tactical situation.

Even German sources are reluctant to produce detailed histories of these two simultaneous campaigns. Even the best (and only true) German history of Hitler's invasion of the West – Karl-Heinz Frieser's *The Blitzkrieg Legend: The 1940 Campaign in the West* (Naval Institute Press: Annapolis, 2012), ignores the conquest of Holland as a mere 'operational deception maneuver' and covers the tank battle at Hannut in a brief eight-page (of 319 pages) passage that is largely a restatement of contemporary 'popular histories'.

The reason *Unternehmen 'F'* lacks coverage is that, although ultimately victorious, the airborne invasion represents a disastrous near-defeat for German forces and, consequently, it is treated as a historically insignificant sideshow. Similarly the tank battle at Hannut, although also victorious, highlights the realities and deficiencies of the panzers (vis-à-vis French mechanized cavalry anyway), whereas the simultaneous and far more decisive victories at Sedan and Dinant – overwhelming French infantry reservists – makes much more flattering press.

As with Osprey Campaign 264: *Fall Gelb (1)*, Peter D. Cornwell's *The Battle of France Then and Now* (Battle of Britain International Limited: London, 2007) and Jean Paul Pallud's *Blitzkrieg in the West: Then and Now* (Battle of Britain International Limited: London, 1991) are without peer the best sources for detailed information about these campaigns. In addition to the sources mentioned here, and those discussed in *Fall Gelb (1)*, the following were important in understanding and describing this complicated campaign:

Belgium: The Official Account of What Happened, 1939–1940, published for the Belgian Ministry of Foreign Affairs by Evans Brothers Limited: London, 1941

Bond, Brian, *France and Belgium 1939–1940*, Associated University Presses, Inc.: Cranbury, NJ, 1979

Cull, Brian, and Bruce Lander with Heinrich Weiss, *Twelve Days in May*, Grub Street: London, 1995

Decker, Cynrik De, and Jean Louis Roba, *Mei 1940 Boven Belgie* ('May 1940 over Belgium'), Uitgeverie De Krijger-Erembodegem, Belgium, 1993

Doorman, Lieutenant-Colonel P. L. G., OBE, *Military Operations of the Dutch Army, 10th–17th May, 1940*, published for the Ministry of Foreign Affairs by George Allen & Unwin Ltd: London, 1944

Kruk, Marek, and Radoslaw Szewczyk, *9. Panzer Division, 1940–1943*, Mushroom Model Publications: Petersfield, UK, 2011

Lucas, James, *Storming Eagles: German Airborne Forces in World War Two*, Arms and Armour: London, 1988

Mallan, K., *Als de Dag van Gisteren: Rotterdam, 10–14 Mei 1940* ('It seems like only yesterday, 10–14 May 1940'), De Gooise Uitgeverij/Unieboek B.V.: Weesp, NL, 1985

Molenaar, Colonel F. J., *Luchtverdediging in de Meidagen 1940* ('Air Defense in the May Days, 1940'), Staatsuitgeverij: 's-Gravenhage, 1970

Morzik, Major General Fritz, *German Air Force Airlift Operations*, Arno Press: New York, 1961

Mrazek, James E., *The Fall of Eben Emael*, Presidio Press: Novato, CA, 1970

Quarrie, Bruce, Osprey Battle Orders 4: *German Airborne Divisions, Blitzkrieg 1940–41*, Osprey Publishing Ltd.: Oxford, 2004

Schoenmaker, Wim and Thijs Postma, *Mei 1940 – de verdediging van het Nederlandse luchtruim* ('May 1940 – The Defence of the Dutch Airspace'), De Bataafsche Leeu: Amsterdam, NL, 1985

Schuurman, J. H., *Vliegveld Bergen NH 1938–1945*, Uitgeverij De Coogh: Bergen, NL, 2001

Sebag-Montefiore, Hugh, *Dunkirk: Fight to the Last Man*, Cambridge, MA: Harvard University Press, 2006

Speidel, General der Flieger Wilhelm, *German Air Force in France and the Low Countries*, USAF Historical Studies No.152, unpublished manuscript (document number K113.107-152) on file at the Air Force Historical Research Center, Maxwell AFB, AL, 1958

Steenbeek, Wilhelmina, *Rotterdam: Invasion of Holland*, Ballantine Books, Inc.: NY, 1973

Thomas, Nigel, PhD., Osprey Men-at-Arms 493: *Hitler's Blitzkrieg Enemies 1940: Denmark, Norway, Netherlands & Belgium*, Osprey Publishing: Oxford, UK, 2014

Weiss, Dr. Heinrich, unpublished manuscript 'Luftkrieg über Holland 10–15 Mai 1940' ('Air War over Holland, 10–15 May 1940'), copy provided to the author by Lt Kol E. H. Brongers

GLOSSARY

AASF	British air force: Advanced Air Striking Force
AéM	Belgian Army air force: *Aéronautique Militaire* or 'military aviation'
AK	German Army: *Armee Korps* or 'army corps'
AOK	German Army: *Armee Oberkommando* or 'army command'
AdA	French air force: *Armée de l'Air* or 'Army of the Air' (Air Force)
ATB	British Army tank brigade
BCC	French Army: *Bataillon de Chars de Combat* or tank battalion.
BEF	British Army: British Expeditionary Force
BEF (AC)	British air force: British Expeditionary Force (Air Component)
BomVA	Dutch Army air force: *Bombardeer Vliegtuig Afdeling* or 'bombardment aircraft unit'
ChA	Belgian Army: *Chasseurs Ardennais* or 'Ardennes light infantry'
DCr	French Army: *Division Cuirassée* or 'armoured division'
DIM	French Army: *Division d'Infanterie Motorisée* or 'motorized infantry division'
DLC	French Army: *Division Légère de Cavalerie* or 'cavalry light division', mixed horse-mounted and mechanized cavalry
DLM	French Army: *Division Légère Mécanique* or 'mechanized light division'
FJR	Luftwaffe paratrooper regiment: *Fallschirmjäger* Regiment
Fliegerkorps	Luftwaffe: 'flying corps', comparable to an army corps
GHQ	British Army: General Headquarters
GQG	French Army: *Grand Quartier Général* or 'general headquarters'
GRDIm	French Army: *Groupe de Reconnaissance de Division d'Infanterie motorisée* or divisional motorized reconnaissance battalion
Heeresgruppe	German Army: 'army group'
Jagdfliegerführer	Luftwaffe: 'fighter flying command'
JaVA	Dutch Army air force: *Jacht Vliegtuig Afdeling* or 'fighter aircraft unit'
JG	Luftwaffe: *Jagdgeschwader* or 'fighter wing'
KG	Luftwaffe: *Kampfgeschwader* or 'battle wing', meaning 'bomber wing'
KM	Dutch Navy: *Koninklijke Marine* or 'Royal Navy'
LG	Luftwaffe: *Lehrgeschwader* or 'instructional wing', for tactics development and training
Luftflotte	Luftwaffe: 'air fleet', equivalent of an army group
LvR	Dutch Army air force: *Luchtvaart Regiment* or 'aviation regiment'
ML	Dutch Army air force: *Militaire Luchtvaart* or 'military aviation'
MLD	Dutch Navy: *Marine Luchtvaartdienst* or 'naval air service'
ObdL	Luftwaffe's command staff: *Oberbefehlshaber der Luftwaffe*
OKH	German Army's command staff: *Oberkommando des Heeres*
OKW	Hitler's personal joint staff: *Oberkommando der Wehrmacht*
PzKpfw	German Army: *Panzer Kampfwagen* or 'armoured battle vehicle', i.e. tank
PzR	German Army: Panzer Regiment
RAF	British air force: Royal Air Force
RAB	German cavalry: *Reiter-Artillerie Bataillon* or 'horse-mounted artillery battalion'
RAD	French medium-calibre (75mm) division-level artillery: *Régiment d'Artillery Divisionaire*
RALD	French division-level heavy-calibre (155mm) artillery: *Régiment d'Artillery Lourde Divisionaire*
RALH	French horse-drawn heavy artillery: *Régiment d'Artillery Lourde Hippomobile*
RATTT	French tractor-drawn artillery: *Régiment d'Artillery Tracté Tout Terrain* or 'all-terrain artillery regiment'
RDP	French Army: *Régiment de Dragons Portés* or lorried infantry regiment assigned to mechanized and cavalry light divisions
RHM	Dutch Army: *Regiment Huzaren Motorrijders* or 'motorcycle-mounted cavalry regiment'
RI	French and Belgian infantry: *Régiment d'Infanterie*
RR	German cavalry: *Reiter Regiment* or 'horse-mounted cavalry regiment'
RTR	British Army: Royal Tank Regiment (source of BEF tank battalions)
RW	Dutch Army: *Regiment Wielrijders* or 'bicycle-mounted light infantry regiment'
Schlachtgruppe	Luftwaffe: 'close air support group'
SdKfz	German Army: *Sondern Kraftfahrzeug* or 'special vehicle', e.g., armoured cars
SOMUA	French Army tank manufacturer: *Société d'Outillage Mécanique et d'Usinage d'Artillerie*
SR	German Army: *Schützen Regiment* or 'motorized rifle regiment'
StG	Luftwaffe: *Stukageschwader* or 'dive-bomber wing'
StratVerVA	Dutch air force: *Strategische Verkennings Vliegtuigen Afdeling* or 'strategic reconnaissance aircraft unit'
TONE	French Army HQ: *Théâtre d'Opérations du Nord-Est* or 'North-East Theatre of Operations'
Veldleger	Dutch Army: 'field army'
ZG	Luftwaffe: *Zerstörergeschwader* or 'destroyer (heavy fighter) wing'

INDEX

References to images are in **bold**.

Printed and bound by CPI Group (UK) Ltd, Croydon, CR0 4YY

21/05/2024

01009009-0014